PUPPY AND DOG TRAINING

ENCYCLOPEDIA

A Complete Guide To Raising, Educating, And Understanding Your Canine Companion

DR. RUBY LUCAS

Table of Content

Chapter 1: Why Train Your Dog?

You're doing great! By picking up a book on dog training, you've already shown yourself to be a responsible and caring pet owner. Congratulations on being a fantastic dog parent—your dog is lucky to have you!

Owning a dog comes with its share of responsibilities. You need to make sure they receive proper healthcare, a nutritious diet, and, equally important, that they learn how to live harmoniously with humans—especially your family.

Although dogs naturally form strong bonds with humans, they aren't born knowing how to live in a human world. Dogs are a different species with their own unique behaviors, which sometimes clash with our expectations of how they should act.

Just as you learned life skills from adults when you were growing up, your dog needs to be taught how to behave in your home and in society. What you were taught as a child may have been a little different from what others learned, but you still gained essential social skills. Now, it's time to teach your dog similar skills.

Your dog doesn't inherently know that it's not okay to pee on your carpet, jump on you, chew your shoes, or dig up your neighbor's garden. He doesn't know what an "indoor voice" is, nor does he realize that it's inappropriate to invade another dog's personal space. These are all things you'll need to teach him—and you absolutely can!

As a responsible pet owner, part of your job is to teach your dog proper manners, clean up after him in public, and make sure he's not a nuisance to others. Training your dog using positive, reward-based methods is the best way to fulfill these responsibilities.

Setting Goals for Training

It's perfectly okay to set goals for your dog's training. Whether you dream of having an agility champion or a therapy dog, you can work toward those goals together. Do your research, learn what's needed to achieve them, and start training your dog accordingly.

However, it's also important to accept your dog for who he is. Not every dog is suited to every task, and every dog is unique. He will never be like any dog you've had in the past, and you won't have another one quite like him again.

Remember, dogs are lifelong companions. Even if your dog never becomes a therapy dog or agility star, he's special in his own way. As you train him, you might find that you need to adjust your expectations based on what you discover about his strengths and challenges. While it can be disappointing to change your goals, remember that your dog's love and companionship are something truly priceless.

Making Time to Train

There is no set time that's perfect for training; the key is finding what works for you and your dog. Are you a morning person? Train your dog when you first wake up. Night owl? Train him in the evenings. The training schedule can be as flexible as you need it to be. The most important thing is to get started and stay consistent.

Many people are busy and may not realize how much work goes into training a dog, especially a puppy. The good news is, positive training doesn't require a lot of time—just about 15 minutes a day. These sessions don't even need to be in one go; you can break them up into short bursts throughout the day.

For example, when you take your dog out for a bathroom break, use that time to practice the "Wait" cue. This means your dog should wait in place until you give him further instructions. Training him this way throughout the day will create a habit, and before long, your dog will naturally wait at the door for your signal.

Establishing House Rules

It's important to set clear house rules before you bring your dog home. If you teach your dog certain behaviors and then change your mind about what's acceptable, it can confuse him. Decide on your rules ahead of time—such as whether you want him on the furniture, in the bedroom, or if it's okay for him to jump on you or kiss your face.

Setting boundaries helps your dog know what's expected of him. It's also crucial to make sure your family or roommates are on the same page, or your dog will get mixed signals. For example, if you don't allow your dog on the bed but your roommate does, your dog will get confused when the rules change depending on who's around.

Chapter 2: Understanding How Dogs Learn

Dogs are a different species with different instincts, so their behaviors can sometimes seem odd to us. For example, if you're out for a walk and your dog suddenly bolts after a squirrel, he's simply responding to his natural instincts. While this doesn't mean you have to tolerate unwanted behaviors, understanding what's normal for dogs can help you train them more effectively.

Instincts and Behaviors

Dogs are born with instincts that lead them to dig, jump, chase, bark, and engage in other typical canine behaviors. If your dog chases a squirrel on a walk, it's simply his natural reaction. Some breeds have been specifically bred for certain tasks—herding livestock, tracking scents, or retrieving game. These instinctive behaviors are hardwired into the dog and are not a sign of disobedience.

For instance, herding breeds like the Collie or Australian Shepherd were bred to move livestock, so it's natural for them to herd things, even children or other pets. While this behavior may not always be desirable, it's essential to understand that your dog isn't being stubborn; he's just responding to his genetic wiring.

Feelings and Emotions

Dogs are emotional beings, just like humans. Studies have shown that dogs have a brain structure similar to ours that allows them to feel emotions like happiness, love, and even anticipation. For example, research by Professor Gregory Berns at Emory University showed that dogs have similar brain activity to humans when reacting to signals of love and food.

Dogs can form deep emotional bonds with their owners, which is why they greet us with such joy after a separation. If you've ever witnessed the reunion between a soldier and their dog, you'll know just how deeply dogs can feel. In fact, dogs may even grieve the loss of another dog.

When it comes to training, this emotional capacity is essential to consider. If dogs can feel pain, it's important not to use harsh methods to train them. Fortunately, positive, reward-based training can help you teach your dog effectively without causing harm.

The Influence of Breed

Your dog's breed (or mix of breeds) has a significant impact on his behavior. Humans have bred dogs for specific purposes—herding, hunting, guarding, or companionship—and these traits are passed down through generations. If your dog is a mixed breed, you might have to guess what behaviors are linked to his genetic background.

For example, herding breeds like the Collie or Border Collie are naturally inclined to chase and herd things, which might include your children or other pets. Sporting breeds, such as Labradors or Golden Retrievers, are often energetic and excel at tasks like retrieving or swimming.

Understanding your dog's breed traits can help you better manage his behavior and tailor your training to suit his natural inclinations.

While you may not always love certain breed-specific behaviors, remember that they are part of your dog's genetic makeup.

Hound Breeds

Hounds were originally bred for hunting. Some, like the Basset Hound, specialize in tracking scents, while others, like the Whippet, hunt using their sight. These breeds are known for their persistence and stamina. Some also have a tendency to bay. Examples of hound breeds include the Greyhound, Bloodhound, Beagle, Irish Wolfhound, and Afghan Hound.

Terrier Breeds

Terriers were developed to hunt and eliminate vermin. They are energetic, persistent, and often feisty. Many have wiry coats that require special grooming techniques, such as stripping, to maintain their appearance. If you've noticed your terrier shaking its toys, it's displaying a common behavior from their hunting instincts. Breeds in this category include the West Highland White Terrier, Parson Russell Terrier, Rat Terrier, Cairn Terrier, and Bull Terrier.

Toy Breeds

Toy breeds were specifically bred to be companions. These small dogs are deeply attached to their owners and often follow them everywhere. Their tiny size makes them ideal for apartment living, but don't tell a Toy breed dog that it's small—it won't believe you! Breeds in this group include the Papillon, Chihuahua, Maltese, Pomeranian, and Pug.

Working Breeds

Working dogs were bred to perform various tasks, such as guarding, pulling sleds, or other labor-intensive duties. Since these jobs vary, the dogs do as well. Generally, working breeds are strong, committed, and often large. Some examples include the Siberian Husky, Saint Bernard, Great Pyrenees, Samoyed, and Great Dane.

Non-Sporting Breeds

The Non-Sporting Group serves as a catch-all category for breeds that don't fit neatly into other classifications. These dogs vary significantly in size and behavior. For instance, the Shiba Inu is a small Japanese dog bred to hunt small wild game, while the Chow Chow is a medium-sized dog from China used for hunting, protection, and herding. Other breeds in this category include the Schipperke, Bichon Frise, and Poodle.

Miscellaneous Group

The AKC's Miscellaneous Group includes purebred dogs that are under consideration for inclusion in regular groups. To be recognized in a regular group, these breeds must have an active parent club and broad breeding activity. Some of these breeds may already be recognized in other countries but haven't yet gained widespread popularity in the U.S.

Understanding Puppy Development

Puppies begin learning almost immediately after birth, making it crucial to understand the early developmental stages of their life.

In the early weeks, puppies learn a great deal from their mother and littermates. For example, the mother licks her puppies to help them urinate and defecate, as well as to keep them clean. If puppies are separated from their mother too soon, they may struggle with house-training later, which is a common issue with puppies bought from pet stores.

Through play, puppies also learn bite inhibition, which helps them understand how to control the force of their bite. If a puppy bites too hard during play, the other puppy will yelp or snap, causing the biter to soften their bite in order to continue playing. These early social lessons are essential for their future interactions. This is why responsible breeders and rescue organizations keep puppies with their families for at least eight weeks.

Puppies raised without siblings, known as singletons, can have challenges. They may not learn proper bite inhibition because there are no littermates to teach them. This can make the pup excessively mouthy, and it may struggle with sharing, since they haven't had to compete for resources like toys or food. If you're raising a singleton puppy, be prepared to invest extra time in training.

Some people consider getting two puppies from the same litter, hoping that they will be great playmates, but this can lead to several issues. Puppies raised together may become overly dependent on one another, making it difficult for them to be comfortable when apart. They may also bond more closely with each other than with their human family members, making training harder. Additionally, as they get older, littermates may develop aggression toward each other, which can become a serious problem.

Raising littermates or two young puppies together can be done, but it requires extra effort and commitment. Each puppy should have its own crate and food bowl, and they should be given individual bonding time with their family members. Training should also be done separately, and each pup should experience individual outings and adventures. While it is possible, the extra workload involved in raising littermates might prove to be more challenging than you expect, which is why many professional trainers advise against getting littermates.

A Long Way from Wolves

Historically, it was believed that dogs evolved directly from wolves, but recent research has cast doubt on this theory. As we learn more about dogs, we're beginning to realize that their evolutionary history might not be as closely tied to wolves as once thought.

Regardless of whether dogs originated from wolves or not, they are now far removed from *Canis lupus*. Imagine a group of Pugs hunting down a caribou—unlikely, right? Over time, humans have shaped dogs into the domestic companions we know and love today, for better or worse.

Why is this important to understand? If you assume your dog behaves like a wolf and respond to it as such, you could be making a serious mistake. Wolves live in packs, which consist of a breeding pair and their offspring. The pack has a hierarchical structure, with an "alpha" male and female at the top and an "omega" at the bottom. Males actively participate in raising the pups.

For a long time, experts thought dogs were also pack animals, but studies of village dogs around the world are challenging this view. Village dogs are those that may have once been pets but now live as strays or semi-feral dogs. They sometimes rely on local people for food but don't live in homes as pets do. These dogs tend to form temporary associations with other dogs, foraging and scavenging together for food. However, they don't form stable packs or cooperate in hunting. Males don't help with rearing the pups, and the dogs are more scavengers than hunters. It's simply not advantageous for them to work together in packs.

If you try to treat your dog like a wolf, you're likely misunderstanding their behavior. For example, if your dog growls when you reach for their collar, you might think they're challenging your authority. You might even try to "correct" them by performing an "alpha roll" and holding them down until they stop struggling. This could backfire badly. A dog might growl in response to a collar grab because it associates that action with something negative or is simply afraid. By forcing them into a distressing situation, you've reinforced their fear, making future interactions more difficult. What you thought was an attempt to assert dominance was actually a sign of discomfort or fear, and now you've created a bigger issue.

Your dog doesn't view you as another dog or a wolf. You don't look or smell like them, so trying to act like one will only confuse or alarm your dog. Dogs communicate through different signals than wolves or other dogs, so trying to mimic canine behavior can lead to misunderstandings and problems.

Early Training and Socialization Benefits

The earlier you start training your dog, the better. Early training helps prevent bad habits from taking root and becoming ingrained. If you properly socialize a puppy during their critical socialization period (up until about 16 weeks of age), you can prevent serious behavioral issues from developing later.

You can begin training your puppy as soon as you bring them home, and the same applies to adolescent and adult dogs. It's never too late to start training! Many people worry that their puppies are too young or their adult dogs too old to learn, but that's not the case.

It's true that your puppy may not be able to attend a group class until they've completed all of their vaccinations, depending on the class requirements. However, you don't need to wait for a class to start training—begin at home. Puppies are like clean slates and tend to learn quickly. Older dogs, while possibly having established habits you'd like to change, usually have better attention spans than easily distracted puppies. Once you show your older dog how enjoyable positive training can be, they'll become a great student.

Chapter 3: Communicating with Your Dog

To effectively train your dog, clear communication is essential. While this may sound simple, it can be challenging to communicate with animals who don't think the way we do.

Many common issues between dogs and humans stem from poor communication. For example, you might want your dog off the couch, but he sees it as the perfect spot to watch the world go by. You expect him to go outside to relieve himself, but he thinks he's being let out to chase squirrels. What you expect may not be what your dog has in mind.

You might assume that your instructions are crystal clear, but the reality is that your dog may not understand you at all. Dogs don't speak human languages. While they can learn to recognize words, you have to teach them what those words mean. For instance, when you say, "Fido, Come!" and he doesn't respond, it's not because he's being stubborn; he simply doesn't understand what you're asking of him. Repeating the command won't help, nor will saying it louder or in a firmer tone. You need to train him to understand the meaning of "Come."

It's also important to note that you don't need to shout or use harsh tones to get your dog to respond. Positive training methods are far more effective, and your dog will respond happily to even soft-spoken cues.

Get the Behavior First, Then Add the Cue

Because dogs don't grasp verbal language right away, it's often more effective to teach the behavior first, and only add the verbal cue once the behavior is consistent. Trying to introduce a verbal command too early can only confuse your dog. You'll naturally want to speak to your dog—it's a human instinct to want to communicate verbally. But remember, your words mean little to your dog until you teach him what they represent.

Once a behavior is consistent, you can pair it with a verbal cue. This process will take some time, as it takes many repetitions for a dog to connect a word to a specific action. Dogs find it harder to learn verbal commands, so be patient and don't expect immediate results. Training sessions should be short, typically just a few minutes at a time, to keep your dog engaged and prevent boredom.

Using Effective Cues

Here are a few tips for communicating with your dog through cues:

- **Keep cues short and clear**: A simple "Come!" is far more effective than "Come over here!"
- **Use one cue for one behavior**: Don't confuse your dog by using the same cue for different actions. For example, don't use "Down" to mean both "stop jumping" and "lie down." This will only confuse him.
- **Be consistent**: Always use the same cue for the same action. If you alternate between "Come!" and "Come here!" your dog will struggle to learn what you're asking. Consistency is key.

- **Use a friendly tone**: Dogs are sensitive to your tone of voice, even if they don't understand your words. Avoid using a stern, no-nonsense tone for every cue. This can make your dog anxious, especially if he's shy or fearful. Save a firmer tone for when it's absolutely necessary, like in situations where your dog is doing something dangerous or inappropriate.

It can be helpful to say your dog's name just before a cue, such as "Fido, Sit," or "Fido, Down." This can be especially useful if you have multiple dogs and need to grab one dog's attention. However, unless you've trained your dog to associate his name with a behavior, simply repeating his name will not help.

For example, if you see a woman in a pet store repeatedly shouting "Buster! Buster! Buster!" at her excited Boxer, this isn't a cue—it's just a name. It won't do anything to communicate what she wants the dog to do unless she's trained him to associate his name with a specific action.

When giving cues, try to say them only once. Repeating a cue teaches your dog that he doesn't need to respond immediately, and that can slow down the learning process. This can be a difficult habit to break, but it's important for your dog to learn that a cue means he needs to respond right away.

Understanding Canine Body Language

One of the most effective ways to understand your dog is through his body language. Dogs have an extensive and detailed vocabulary of body movements and signals that they use to communicate with one another. By learning to read these signs, you'll better understand your dog's feelings and intentions.

Ears

- **Ears flat against the head**: This typically indicates fear.
- **Ears forward**: This shows interest or excitement. However, some breeds, like Cocker Spaniels, may have ears that naturally lay flat and don't show much expression.

Eyes

- **Soft eyes**: A relaxed, content dog may have soft, squinty eyes.
- **Direct eye contact**: Dogs don't always interpret eye contact as a challenge. In fact, it's usually a sign of confidence or friendly connection. A shy or nervous dog may avoid eye contact.

Mouth

- **Smiling**: Some dogs smile, a clear sign of happiness.
- **Tense or closed mouth**: This can signal stress or discomfort. A dog that's panting might simply be tired, but panting can also indicate fear or anxiety.
- **Snarling or lip curling**: This is a warning sign. A dog will do this if he's feeling threatened. Be cautious and respectful of the dog's boundaries.

Tail

- **Tail tucked under**: This signals fear.

- **Wagging tail**: While many people think a wagging tail always means a friendly dog, this isn't always true. A rapidly wagging tail can indicate anxiety or excitement. A high, stiff wagging tail might suggest aggression or arousal.

Overall Body Posture

- **Weight distribution**: If a dog shifts his weight backward, he's likely trying to increase the distance between himself and something that's scaring him. If he leans forward, he's eager or interested.
- **Curved body**: This generally indicates friendliness and submission.
- **Play bow**: A dog lowers his front end, keeping his rear end up, as an invitation to play.
- **Stiff, threatening posture**: If a dog is tense with a hard stare and stiffened body, he is likely feeling threatened and may escalate to aggression.

Recognizing Signs of Stress

A dog's body language can tell you a lot about whether he's feeling stressed, anxious, or fearful. Recognizing these signs is essential to ensuring successful training and maintaining your dog's well-being. If your dog is showing signs of stress, it's important to stop the training session and address his emotional state, as a stressed dog cannot learn effectively.

Some signs of stress in dogs include:

- **Licking lips**
- **Yawning**

- **Cowering**
- **Trembling or quivering**
- **Whining**
- **Shaking off (similar to when wet)**
- **Tucking tail**
- **Turning away or trying to escape**
- **Flattening ears**
- **Sweaty paw prints (dogs sweat through their paws)**

Context is important when reading these signs. If your dog is at the vet and showing some of these signs, it may simply be stress from the environment. But if your dog is displaying multiple stress signals in other contexts, it's important to recognize that he may be uncomfortable or scared.

Understanding Displacement Signals and Dog Behavior in Context

Dogs are incredibly intuitive animals, and much of their communication relies on body language and subtle signals. Often, we may observe a dog displaying a behavior that seems out of context for the situation at hand. These behaviors are normal, but they might appear odd or disconnected from the surrounding circumstances. Such actions are known as **displacement signals** or **cutoff signals**, and they can be key indicators of stress, discomfort, or confusion.

What Are Displacement Signals?

A **displacement signal** is a behavior that occurs in response to a situation that is causing stress or confusion for the dog. Essentially, these signals are a way for the dog to cope with the emotions that arise from a particular situation. They often manifest in actions that seem unrelated or out of context, which can be confusing for humans. However, understanding these signals is critical for interpreting the dog's emotional state.

One common example of a displacement signal is when a dog, feeling nervous or stressed, starts to **sniff the floor**. While this may seem like a routine behavior, it can actually be a sign that the dog is attempting to avoid eye contact or redirect their attention to something less threatening. For instance, imagine your friend brings over a new puppy to meet your dog. As the puppy enters the house, your dog excitedly rushes over to greet him, but instead of continuing the greeting, the puppy suddenly begins sniffing the floor. In this context, the sniffing is not about curiosity or exploration; it is a displacement behavior. The puppy could be signaling to your dog that he is not a threat, and by avoiding direct eye contact, he is trying to de-escalate the situation. Alternatively, the puppy may feel overwhelmed by the boisterous greeting and needs to momentarily retreat into a more neutral activity to calm himself.

Your Body Language and Its Impact on Your Dog

Just as dogs communicate with you using body language, humans also send signals through their own physical behavior. Your body language can influence your dog's responses and interactions with you. Interestingly, you may unintentionally convey messages that you did not mean to send, especially if you're unaware of how your movements or posture can affect the dog.

Intimidating Movements and Posture

For example, **looming over a dog** can be perceived as threatening, especially for dogs that are fearful or more sensitive. Some dogs may not mind having a person stand tall above them, but others could see this as a sign of aggression or dominance. When training or interacting with your dog, it's essential to maintain a neutral and non-threatening posture.

Bending over at the waist and calling your dog to come to you may cause the dog to hesitate or stay at a distance, as they may feel intimidated by your looming position. On the other hand, if you crouch down, bending at the knees and bringing yourself to the dog's level, your dog is likely to feel more comfortable and may approach you more willingly.

Emotional States Reflected in Body Language

Your mood also plays a significant role in your dog's response to you. Dogs are incredibly perceptive and can pick up on the smallest changes in your body language. When you're angry or upset, your body becomes stiffer, your voice changes tone, and your gestures may become more abrupt. While you may feel like you're maintaining control, your dog can sense the tension, and this can make training sessions less productive.

A stressed dog may respond to this shift in energy by becoming more excitable or, conversely, retreating. The more frustrated or tense you become, the more likely your dog will act in ways that exacerbate the situation, such as bouncing around or becoming distracted. It's crucial to stay calm and composed during training or any interaction with your dog to ensure a positive outcome.

The Dangers of Staring

Direct eye contact is another example of a communication barrier. While humans use eye contact as a sign of engagement and affection, for dogs, staring can be interpreted as a challenge. It can be especially concerning when children attempt to cradle a dog's face and stare directly into their eyes. For some dogs, this may be unsettling and may trigger an aggressive response, especially if the dog feels cornered or unable to escape the situation. It's essential to teach children how to properly approach and interact with dogs, avoiding overly intense eye contact or close face-to-face encounters.

Hands Over Words: The Power of Hand Signals

Dogs rely heavily on body language to communicate, and this extends to how they understand commands. **Hand signals** or other physical cues are often easier for dogs to grasp than verbal commands. Since dogs are naturally adept at reading body language, they tend to focus more on the movements of your hands, arms, and posture rather than just the words you say.

When training your dog with hand signals, consistency is key. For example, if you're teaching your dog to lie down, you may use a downward motion with your hand to signal the command. However, if one day you change the motion or keep your hand at your side instead of pointing down, your dog may not understand what you're asking of him. This doesn't mean your dog is being defiant; it simply means they are confused by the inconsistency in your signals.

It's also important to note that hand signals don't always need to be large or exaggerated. You can gradually "fade" the signal, making it more subtle over time as your dog becomes more accustomed to the command.

Understanding a Dog's Sensory World

A dog's senses are far more acute than those of humans. This is particularly important when it comes to understanding why your dog might get distracted during training, while walking, or in new environments. Their sensory perception is finely tuned, allowing them to detect things that you might not even be aware of. Let's break down the key senses that affect how dogs interact with the world.

The Nose: A Dog's Most Powerful Sense

A dog's sense of smell is truly extraordinary. It's estimated that a dog's sense of smell is **10,000 to 100,000 times** more sensitive than ours. Dogs have up to **300 million olfactory receptors** in their noses, compared to the 6 million that humans have. The area of the brain that processes smells is also much larger in dogs, accounting for a significant portion of their brain's overall function.

Dogs have a unique way of processing smells. When they inhale, the air is split into two separate pathways—one for breathing and one dedicated entirely to smelling. Approximately 12% of the air a dog inhales goes to a recessive part of the nose for scent detection. This allows them to keep sniffing continuously while still breathing normally.

Additionally, dogs possess **Jacobson's organ**, also known as the vomeronasal organ, which is used to detect pheromones. These are chemical signals that animals produce to communicate with others, especially for mating purposes. This organ allows dogs to detect pheromones that humans cannot perceive, adding an extra layer of sensory information that influences their behavior.

Because of their remarkable sense of smell, dogs are often used in scent-based activities, such as **tracking**, **search and rescue**, and even **medical detection**. They can identify specific scents, such as drugs, explosives, or even cancer, far more accurately than humans.

Vision: More Than Just Black and White

For many years, it was believed that dogs could only see in black and white, but recent studies have shown that dogs may actually have some degree of **color vision**. Their ability to see colors is not as vivid or as wide-ranging as ours, but they can distinguish between certain shades, particularly blue and yellow.

Dogs are believed to have a more limited spectrum of color vision because they possess fewer **cone photoreceptors** in their retinas than humans. While humans have three types of cones that allow us to see a wide range of colors, dogs only have two, meaning they likely perceive colors like **red and green** as shades of gray or brown.

Furthermore, dogs' eyes are positioned on the sides of their heads, which gives them a **wider field of vision** (about 240 degrees), compared to humans, who have around 200 degrees. However, this also means that dogs have a **reduced field of binocular vision** (the ability to focus both eyes on a single object). As a result, dogs can see things at a distance, but they often need to get closer to objects to clearly define them.

The Ears: Acute Hearing

Dogs also possess an incredibly sharp sense of hearing. They can hear sounds at much higher frequencies than humans can, allowing them to detect things we cannot even perceive. Dogs' ears are equipped with about **18 muscles** that allow them to move their ears independently, helping them pinpoint the source of a sound.

A dog's **ear canal** is also different from ours—it's **L-shaped**, which means that it's harder to examine the ear canal directly without specialized equipment. This unique structure, along with floppy or drop ears, can create a more conducive environment for ear infections, so it's important to take care of a dog's ears, especially if they are prone to infections.

Taste and Touch: More Than Meets the Eye

While dogs don't have as many taste buds as humans (around **1,700 compared to our 9,000**), their sense of **touch** is incredibly sensitive. Dogs have specialized hairs called **vibrissac** around their faces, which allow them to detect even the slightest changes in the air around them. These tactile sensors are crucial for navigating the world, especially in low-light conditions.

When it comes to **petting**, not all dogs enjoy the same type of touch. Some may love having their ears scratched, while others prefer having their rear end rubbed. Some dogs may not enjoy petting at all, particularly if they were not socialized to it as puppies. It's important to respect a dog's preferences and only engage in petting behaviors that they enjoy.

Understanding the nuanced world of dog behavior and sensory perception can greatly enhance our ability to communicate with our canine companions. Displacement signals, body language, and the use of hand signals are just a few of the ways dogs express themselves, and being attuned to these signs allows us to respond appropriately to their emotional needs. By recognizing the power of a dog's senses—especially their exceptional sense of smell, hearing, and touch—we can create better environments for them to thrive in, whether we're training, walking, or simply enjoying each other's company.

Chapter 4: Focus on the Positive!

Science-based positive training methods are incredibly effective. They work with all types of dogs, including those that may be labeled as "stubborn" or "difficult." Positive training is particularly beneficial for shy or fearful dogs, and it can be used with dogs of all sizes—whether big or small, young puppies or older dogs, energetic dogs or laid-back ones. This success is due to the fact that these methods adhere to the core principles of learning. Positive training is universal and can be used with any species, as proven by its widespread use with wild animals. For example, animal trainers have successfully used positive reinforcement to teach large, potentially dangerous animals like elephants and tigers to cooperate. If these animals can be trained to safely perform behaviors like offering their feet for care or sitting calmly for medical procedures, you can certainly train your dog without resorting to force or intimidation.

Here are some key benefits of positive training:

- **No need for physical strength:** You don't have to rely on physical power to train your dog. Positive methods don't involve forcing your dog into positions or using physical pressure. This opens up training to people of various physical abilities, including allowing children (with supervision) to train the dog as well.
- **Efficiency:** Positive training is quick and effective. Training sessions only need to last a few minutes, which is especially beneficial for puppies or dogs with short attention spans. This is also perfect for people with busy schedules, as even a few minutes multiple times a day can yield great progress.

- **Fast results:** Dogs enjoy positive training and will eagerly engage with you, leading to faster learning and better retention of commands.
- **Motivation to work for you:** Positive training fosters a strong relationship between you and your dog, as they will want to work for you, not because they fear punishment, but because they find the experience rewarding.
- **Fun for both of you:** Training doesn't have to be a chore. By using positive methods, both you and your dog can enjoy the process of learning together.

It's important to note that using positive training doesn't mean letting your dog get away with bad behavior. "Positive" does not equate to "permissive." You should set clear rules and boundaries and have realistic expectations for your dog's behavior. Positive training allows you to establish these guidelines without being harsh or punitive.

The Science Behind Training

The positive training techniques discussed in this guide are grounded in science, specifically in learning theory developed by psychologists and behaviorists. If you've taken a psychology course, you may recognize some of these principles. Because these methods are scientifically validated, they have consistently proven effective across different contexts and species. In fact, these techniques work on any animal with a nervous system.

Scientists have applied these principles to laboratory animals, where animals perform tasks and are rewarded with food when they do so correctly. This reinforcement causes them to repeat the task more frequently.

These methods are also used by wild animal and marine mammal trainers. For example, trainers teach performance behaviors and husbandry tasks (such as getting a whale to roll for an ultrasound or training a wolf to remain still for medical treatment) using positive reinforcement. These techniques have even been used to train gorillas to voluntarily present their arms for insulin shots. Similarly, pet owners use these methods to train dogs, birds, horses, and even cats. While there's a wealth of research on canine behavior, understanding classical and operant conditioning is enough to train your dog effectively.

Classical Conditioning

Classical conditioning involves associating a neutral stimulus with an involuntary response until the stimulus triggers that response. A neutral stimulus is something that doesn't evoke any response from the animal initially. An involuntary response, on the other hand, is something the animal does naturally, without thinking about it.

A famous example of classical conditioning is Ivan Pavlov's experiment with dogs. Pavlov discovered that dogs would salivate not just when they saw food, but when they saw the lab assistant who typically fed them. Over time, they learned to associate the presence of the assistant with food, and their salivation became a conditioned response to his arrival.

In a similar way, you may have experienced classical conditioning with your dog. The first time your dog saw a leash, it was just a neutral object to him. But after repeatedly associating the leash with going for walks, your dog likely began to get excited when he saw it. The leash went from being a neutral stimulus to a conditioned stimulus that triggered the involuntary response of excitement.

Operant Conditioning

Operant conditioning involves changing an animal's behavior by manipulating the consequences that follow it. Behaviors are either reinforced or punished, which affects whether they occur more or less frequently.

There are four main types of operant conditioning: positive reinforcement, positive punishment, negative reinforcement, and negative punishment. The terms "positive" and "negative" here do not mean "good" or "bad," but rather refer to whether something is added or removed following a behavior.

- **Positive Reinforcement**: Adding something pleasant after a behavior to increase its frequency. For example, giving your dog a treat when he comes when called encourages him to repeat the behavior.
- **Positive Punishment**: Adding something unpleasant after a behavior to decrease its frequency. For instance, if you call your dog and yell at him when he comes, he may be less likely to come when called in the future.
- **Negative Reinforcement**: Removing something unpleasant after a behavior to increase its frequency. An example is if your dog has a thorn in his paw and you remove it after he comes to you, making him more likely to come to you when called in the future.
- **Negative Punishment**: Removing something pleasant after a behavior to decrease its frequency. For instance, if your dog is chewing a bone and you take it away when he doesn't respond to a cue, he may be less likely to ignore the cue in the future.

In general, positive training focuses on the use of positive reinforcement and negative punishment. For example, if your dog sits when you ask, you reward him with praise or a treat (positive reinforcement). On the other hand, if your dog jumps on you and you ignore him (removing your attention), the behavior is less likely to occur again (negative punishment).

Training Behaviors Step-by-Step

A **cue** is the word or signal you use to ask your dog to perform a specific behavior. To get your dog to perform a behavior reliably on cue, you first need to teach that behavior. The following steps will guide you through the process of teaching and reinforcing a new behavior with your dog.

Step 1: Achieving the Behavior

There are several effective techniques to encourage a dog to perform a specific behavior, including luring, shaping, capturing, and modeling.

Luring/Targeting

Luring and targeting are hands-off methods of guiding a dog through a behavior. For example, you can use a treat in your hand to lure the dog into a "down" position by lowering the treat and allowing the dog to follow it. Alternatively, you can teach the dog to touch his nose to your hand, using it as a target. This method is effective for teaching behaviors like coming to you, getting on and off furniture, or entering and exiting the car.

Luring and targeting are commonly used techniques and often provide quick results, especially if the dog is motivated. However, to be successful, the lure must be highly appealing to the dog; otherwise, the dog may lose interest. If your dog ignores the lure or loses focus during training, you may need to switch to a more enticing treat.

In luring, it's important to phase out the lure quickly. For example, after successfully luring the dog into a down position three times, try the same motion without holding a treat. Even without the treat in your hand, your dog should still follow your hand gesture. Once the dog performs the behavior, mark it (with a click or verbal cue) and reward him. The goal is to phase out the lure before eliminating rewards.

This isn't about tricking the dog. Dogs have an incredible sense of smell, so they can tell if there's no treat in your hand. What they are learning is the hand signal. If you always use a treat, the dog may only lie down when you have food in your hand. To avoid this dependency, be sure to reduce the use of treats early on.

Shaping

Shaping involves reinforcing successive approximations of a desired behavior. For example, to teach a dog to "settle" on his bed, you might first reward him for looking at the bed, then for moving towards it, sniffing it, placing one paw on it, and so on, until he eventually lies down on the bed. Each small step in the process is reinforced.

Shaping is effective because it teaches the dog to pay close attention to the cues you're providing. It also encourages problem-solving, which may lead to longer-lasting learning. For instance, when you have to navigate a new route, you may hesitate or make mistakes, but once you drive the route yourself, you learn it more effectively.

Shaping is particularly useful for fearful dogs who may be hesitant to approach you for luring. It also provides a great opportunity to build a positive relationship through rewarding successive behaviors. Moreover, shaping is an ideal method for teaching behaviors that the dog would not naturally perform, such as retrieving items like keys or remote controls, or even service dog tasks like turning lights on and off.

Capturing

Capturing is the method of marking and reinforcing a behavior that the dog performs naturally, without any prompts. For example, if your dog lies down and crosses his paws, you can mark and reward that behavior when it occurs. Over time, the dog will start doing it more often. Once the behavior is reliable, you can introduce a cue to prompt the behavior on command. Capturing is great for teaching unique or quirky behaviors that might be difficult to lure, like head tilting, shaking off water, or stretching.

Modeling

Modeling involves physically guiding the dog into the desired position, but this method is less commonly used. It may not be necessary since behaviors can often be achieved using simpler techniques. Additionally, modeling can be challenging for some people. For example, it might be difficult for a small person to physically move a large dog into the sitting position. Modeling doesn't engage the dog as much, as you're doing most of the work for him. It's also not ideal for shy or fearful dogs because physical manipulation can be unsettling for them.

Step 2: Marking and Rewarding the Behavior

Marker training is a highly effective positive reinforcement technique. A marker, such as a clicker, is used to signal the precise moment the dog performs the desired behavior. The click sound is distinct and easily recognizable by dogs. After marking the behavior, you immediately provide a reward. The click signifies that a treat or other reward is coming, teaching the dog to work for the marker sound.

While a clicker is commonly used, you can also use a verbal marker, but it should be a short, clear word that is not used in casual conversation. A phrase like "good dog" is too long to be an effective marker, as the dog might complete multiple behaviors before you finish saying it.

It's important to distinguish between marking and praising. Marking immediately communicates to the dog that he has done something you like, while praise comes after the behavior and is part of the reward process.

There are several benefits to using a marker:

- **Clarity and Precision**: A marker provides clear communication about the exact behavior being reinforced.
- **Distinct Sound**: Clickers produce a unique sound, making it easy for the dog to recognize when they are being marked.
- **Consistency**: The sound of the click is the same every time, making it predictable for the dog.

- **Non-judgmental**: The click is neutral and doesn't carry any emotional weight.
- **Transferability**: Once your dog associates the click with a reward, anyone can use it to mark the behavior.

Timing is key when using a marker. If you're new to this type of training, be patient with yourself as you learn. It may take some time to get the timing right, but with practice, you'll improve. One of the advantages of marker training is that even if you don't get the timing perfect, you can easily correct it and avoid causing harm or confusion, unlike punishment-based training methods.

Tips for Using a Clicker Effectively:

- **Don't point the clicker at your dog**—it's not a remote control.
- **Click only once per behavior** to mark the specific action.
- **Use the clicker solely for marking behaviors**—don't use it to grab the dog's attention.
- **Always follow the click with a reward**. Even if you click at the wrong time, give the dog a reward to maintain the value of the clicker.
- **Remember, the click ends the behavior**. After marking a behavior like "down," it's fine if the dog gets up to receive the treat.

The Ten Rules of Shaping

1. Gradually increase criteria in small steps so the dog always has a chance to succeed.
2. Focus on one aspect of the behavior at a time—avoid trying to shape two things simultaneously.

3. Use a variable-reinforcement schedule for the current behavior before raising the criteria.
4. Relax old criteria temporarily when introducing a new one.
5. Plan ahead—be prepared for unexpected progress and know what to reinforce next.
6. Avoid switching trainers in the middle of shaping a behavior. Stick with one person for consistency.
7. If a shaping procedure isn't working, try a different approach.
8. Avoid unnecessary interruptions during training to prevent accidental punishment.
9. If behavior starts to deteriorate, review the basics and reinforce small, easily earned behaviors.
10. End training sessions on a positive note, leaving the dog with a sense of success.

,Step 3: Introduce a Cue

Once the behavior is reliable, meaning your dog consistently performs the action, it's time to introduce a cue. This cue could either be a word or a physical signal that prompts your dog to execute the behavior.

Why wait to add the cue? Why not simply say "Down" and lure your dog into the down position? Because it's actually harder for dogs to learn that way. Dogs don't understand English, so saying "Down" has no inherent meaning for them. Repeating the word over and over won't help either. Think about it: If someone speaks to you in a language you don't understand and keeps repeating the words, does that make it easier for you to comprehend? Of course not. The same applies to your dog. That's why it's best to first teach the behavior, and then attach the cue to it.

For stationary behaviors like "Sit," "Down," or "Settle," it's also helpful to introduce a release cue. This tells your dog that it's okay to move from the position. Without a release cue, the dog might either stay in position indefinitely or get up at random times. By teaching a release cue, you'll help your dog maintain a longer, more consistent "Stay." You can use the same release cue for all stationary behaviors, as it consistently signals that the dog can stop holding the position. Pick a word that you don't use often in everyday conversation, like "Okay," "Free," or "Release." The exact word doesn't matter, as long as you're consistent with its usage.

Step 4: Train to Fluency

Once your dog responds reliably to the cue, it's time to train the behavior to fluency. This means your dog should perform the behavior reliably, even with distractions, in different environments, and under varying conditions. It's not useful if your dog only responds well in your living room. If that's the only place you train, then that's likely the only place the dog will perform the behavior consistently.

For example, you may have taught your dog to "Sit-Stay" at home. But when you take them to the park and cue "Sit, Stay," the dog might sit briefly, then jump up and run off after a squirrel. This is common because you haven't trained the behavior with the distractions of an outdoor environment or something as tempting as a squirrel.

The same applies to house training. Just because your dog doesn't eliminate in your home doesn't mean they won't do so at a friend's house. So, when you visit a relative's home, your dog might pee on the carpet despite being well-trained at home. This can be due to excitement, stress, or a lack of training in new locations.

To train a behavior to fluency, you need to work gradually. Start with a few small distractions, and as your dog gets better, add more. Keep training sessions short, and if your dog starts struggling, it likely means you're advancing too quickly. Go back to a level where your dog was successful, practice there, and then slowly increase the challenge.

You can introduce distractions to your training in many ways. At first, train in a calm, familiar space, like your living room. Once the behavior is reliable, start adding distractions like moving around, changing your position, or having other people or animals nearby. Gradually introduce more complex distractions, such as moving farther away from your dog, changing locations, or even dropping objects. If you're working on "Sit-Stay," for example, start by taking a single step away, and then gradually add more steps. Avoid jumping from standing next to your dog to being across the room, as that could overwhelm them.

Training to fluency takes time, especially depending on your dog's age and personality. Puppies, for instance, have short attention spans and get distracted easily by even small things, like a ladybug. Similarly, certain breeds (e.g., Boxers or Labradors) may be naturally more energetic and distracted. Be patient and progress at your dog's pace. Training will be worth the effort. By increasing distractions and practicing in different environments, your dog will eventually perform reliably no matter the situation.

Think of therapy dogs, for example, who need to remain calm in busy places like hospitals or emotionally charged settings such as hospice care. Search and rescue dogs must perform under difficult conditions, with loud noises and challenging smells. Police dogs must work in environments ranging from schools to dark alleys. Achieving this level of performance doesn't happen overnight. It requires consistent training to fluency, ensuring the dog can perform reliably no matter what's going on around them.

Reward-Based Training

If someone offered you chocolate chip cookies, ice cream, or tiramisu, you might have a preference. Perhaps cold foods bother your teeth, so ice cream wouldn't appeal to you. Maybe you don't enjoy coffee, so tiramisu wouldn't excite you either. Or perhaps you simply don't like chocolate. Everyone has different preferences when it comes to food, and dogs are no different.

Not all dogs love being petted. Some may tolerate it, but others are enthusiastic about it. Some dogs are crazy about fetch, while others couldn't care less. Some will eat anything you give them, while others are quite picky.

When using reward-based training, it's essential to identify what your dog finds rewarding. The rewards you use must be appealing to your dog specifically.

To determine this, make a list of your dog's preferences. This will help you especially when working with distractions or teaching more complex behaviors. For instance, some dogs may struggle with lying down. If a regular food treat doesn't entice them to do it, you may need to try a higher-ranked reward from your list.

A common question with reward-based training is, "When do I stop using rewards?" While building a behavior, rewards are essential. Once the behavior is fluent and your dog consistently performs it under various conditions, you can start gradually reducing the use of rewards. However, many people make the mistake of removing rewards too early, which can cause the behavior to deteriorate. It's important to phase out rewards only when your dog reliably performs the behavior, even with distractions and in different environments.

There's a significant difference between a reward and a bribe. A reward is given after the correct behavior, while a bribe is used to prompt the behavior. You never want to bribe your dog, as this can make them dependent on the bribe and less likely to perform the behavior without it. For instance, if you want your dog to get off the couch, you can give the cue "Off!" and reward them when they do it. This is a reward.

If, instead, you tempt your dog with a treat to get them off the couch and only give them the treat once they comply, that's a bribe. If you do this too often, your dog will only get off the couch when they see the treat, not when they hear the cue. You want to use rewards to reinforce behaviors, not bribes.

Attention and Affection

Most dogs enjoy receiving attention, though not all are fond of physical affection like petting. For example, many dogs don't enjoy being petted on the top of their head, as this is perceived as an assertive gesture. As a result, they might duck away or avoid your hand. However, some dogs don't mind it at all.

When interacting physically with your dog, it's important to pay attention to their body language. Does your dog stiffen up? Do their ears flatten, or do they look worried? Do they pull away or struggle? These are signs that your dog is not comfortable with the interaction. On the other hand, if your dog leans into you, relaxes, and squints their eyes, they are likely enjoying the affection.

If you love to cuddle with your dog but they don't seem to enjoy it, it's crucial to respect their boundaries. Forcing physical affection on a dog who doesn't like it can lead to negative behavior like growling, snapping, or biting. This is especially common with children who may not recognize when a dog is uncomfortable. Make sure to observe your dog's cues to determine if they're enjoying the attention.

For dogs who love physical interaction, learn what they enjoy the most—whether it's a belly rub, a scratch behind the ears, or a chest rub. These can make great rewards during training.

Verbal Praise

Verbal praise can be useful when you don't have a more valuable reward available, but dogs generally don't appreciate it as much as humans do. While a person may feel pleased by a compliment, dogs tend to prefer tangible rewards like treats. If you give your dog a choice between verbal praise and a treat, they will likely choose the treat.

This doesn't mean that your dog doesn't love you or that you're a bad pet owner. It's simply normal for dogs to be more motivated by food. When using verbal praise effectively, however, make sure to use a warm, enthusiastic tone. If your dog responds positively with relaxed body language, you're on the right track.

Food Rewards

Food is one of the most effective and motivating rewards for most dogs. It can be particularly useful for teaching new behaviors. When using food as a reward, ensure the pieces are small and easy to swallow, as large treats can slow down training by interrupting the flow of repetitions.

Treats with strong smells are more appealing to dogs. At home, you can use your dog's regular kibble for training if they are motivated by it. This can help control their daily food intake and prevent obesity. For example, if you feed your dog 2 cups of kibble a day, you can use part of it for training throughout the day, which can also make your dog work for their meals.

If you're training in a more distracting environment, such as a dog class, you might need to use higher-value treats. Regular kibble might not be enough to grab your dog's attention amidst distractions like other dogs and people.

When selecting commercial dog treats, choose healthy options with natural ingredients. Avoid treats filled with artificial colors and sugars, as they are unnecessary and can harm your dog's health.

Toys

Toys can serve as enjoyable rewards for some dogs, though others may not be as interested in them. Some dogs are excited by fetch toys, while others prefer tug toys or have a particular attachment to a ball. If you use toys as rewards, keep in mind that training sessions might take longer since you'll need to allow time for play. This can be a challenge in the early stages of training when quick repetitions are needed.

Always choose safe toys. Avoid small chew toys that could be swallowed, as well as tennis balls, which can damage a dog's teeth if chewed excessively.

Play

Games like chase, hide-and-seek, and recall can also serve as fun and effective rewards during training. These activities provide breaks during training sessions, especially if your dog becomes frustrated. For example, playing chase with your dog can help teach them a fast "Come" command, especially if you encourage them to chase you rather than the other way around.

Life Rewards

Life rewards are activities your dog enjoys, and these can be powerful motivators. Does your dog love sniffing? Let them have a sniffing session as a reward. Does your dog love car rides or swimming? These activities can also be used as rewards. While life rewards aren't always practical during every training session, using them occasionally can make a significant impact.

Introducing the Clicker

Before you begin formal training, it's important to teach your dog the meaning of the clicker. The click sound needs to be associated with the arrival of a treat. This is the first exercise you should complete before moving on to other training tasks.

1. Get five small, tasty treats and be close to your dog (not across the yard).
2. Click once, then immediately give your dog a treat. Repeat this five times.
3. Practice this exercise twice a day for two days.

In no time, your dog will start to associate the sound of the click with a treat, and you'll be ready to use the clicker for training.

Introducing a Target

Targeting is a useful training skill. There are two primary types of targets—nose targets and paw targets. A nose target, such as touching your hand, can lead to a variety of behaviors, including recall or teaching your dog to get on or off furniture. A paw target can help teach your dog to go to their bed or stay out of the kitchen. Here's how to introduce your dog to a nose target:

1. Hold your hand an inch from your dog's nose, with the palm facing downward.
2. When your dog touches their nose to your hand, click and reward with a treat.
3. Repeat this for ten repetitions, and end the session.
4. After your dog consistently touches your hand, start moving your hand to different positions, such as to the left and right of their nose.
5. Once your dog is reliably following your hand, add the verbal cue "Touch" just before presenting your hand.

Continue to practice and gradually increase the difficulty by having your dog follow your hand at greater distances.

With patience and consistency, your dog will learn to respond to these cues and behaviors, strengthening your training sessions.

Introducing a Paw Target

Select a target that your dog can touch with their paw. Be aware that some dogs are quite enthusiastic with their paws, so choose a durable target. A drink coaster or a lid from a margarine tub are good options. Here's how to teach your dog to touch a paw target:

Goal: Your dog will touch their paw to the target. **What You'll Need:** Clicker, treats, paw target.

1. Place the target on the ground near your dog. If your dog reaches out with their paw to touch the target, immediately click, remove the target, and give them a treat. However, this isn't very common. Most dogs will explore the target with their nose first. If your dog noses the target, click, remove the target, and treat. You remove the target so your dog doesn't touch it again before you are ready to click and reward.

Why click for nosing the target instead of pawing? Nosing and pawing are closely linked behaviors for dogs. If your dog starts by using their nose, don't worry—they'll quickly switch to pawing.

2. If your dog begins pawing the target, repeat the action about ten times, then end the training session.

3. If your dog initially noses the target, continue until they reliably nose the target about ten times. Then, present the target and wait. Don't click for nosing anymore. They will likely get frustrated, and this will encourage them to try pawing. The moment they touch the target with their paw, click, remove the target, and treat. Repeat this process ten more times, then end the session.

Tip: Some dogs are more paw-oriented and will quickly pick up this behavior, while others may take longer. Training a paw target may only require one session or several. Keep progressing at your dog's pace. Also, some dogs may try to pick up the target, especially sporting breeds. If this happens, anchor the target with your foot to prevent it from being picked up. Remember, this is not a retrieve exercise. Allowing your dog to pick up the target will make it harder for them to learn to paw it.

Once your dog is consistently pawing the target, it's time to move on to the next step.

1. Start placing the target in different locations, but within a couple of feet (around one meter) of your dog. Click and treat every time your dog touches the target with their paw.
2. Hold the target in the palm of your hand, flat against the ground. Click and treat for every correct response.
3. Gradually raise the target a little higher, but keep it at a comfortable height for your dog. Click and treat for every correct response.
4. Repeat this process for about ten repetitions and then end the training session.

Once your dog is reliably pawing the target regardless of where it's placed, it's time to add a cue.

1. Just before presenting the target, say the cue "Paw" in a friendly tone. When your dog paws the target, click and treat.
2. Repeat this sequence for ten repetitions. End the session.

This method will help your dog learn to associate the cue "Paw" with the behavior of touching the target with their paw.

Chapter 5: Early Training

Puppyhood is a special, endearing, chaotic, and sometimes frustrating period in a dog's life. When you bring your tiny, adorable puppy home, you may envision a future where he becomes the perfect companion—loving, protective of your family, and always obedient. You dream of a dog who will excel in obedience training, agility, and possibly even become a therapy dog. You picture him never chewing on your shoes, soiling the carpet, or misbehaving in any way. You expect nothing less than perfection.

However, how your puppy reaches these goals depends on both his innate temperament and, most crucially, on how you and everyone around him guide and interact with him.

From the moment you meet your puppy, you begin to bond with him. It's essential to start training right away—ideally when he's around eight weeks old. Puppies should remain with their mothers and littermates until at least this age to learn crucial social skills that will help them grow into well-adjusted adult dogs. Be cautious if a breeder offers to send a puppy home with you earlier than eight weeks.

Young puppies are like sponges when it comes to learning, but they have short attention spans. As a result, training sessions should be brief—just a couple of minutes at a time. While you're teaching your puppy new behaviors, you'll also be helping him become comfortable with human interaction. The positive reinforcement of treats will teach him that hands approaching him are a good thing, which will make future grooming, handling, and even picking him up easier. Training sessions will also make you more fun to be around, helping to deepen your bond and build trust.

Essential Training Equipment

There are many products you can buy for your puppy, and it's tempting to fill your cart at the pet store. However, there are specific items you'll need to support your puppy's training journey.

Leash

Choose a 4- to 6-foot leash made of nylon, cotton, or leather. Avoid retractable leashes, as they are more suited for exercising or advanced training but don't offer the control needed for basic walking or training. Even when locked, they don't provide enough flexibility or control. If you drop the leash, the plastic handle can chase your puppy, potentially frightening him.

Make sure the leash is appropriately sized for your puppy. For a small dog, a ¼-inch-thick leash with a small clasp works best. Larger puppies require a sturdier leash (¾-inch to 1-inch thick). Avoid leashes that are thin but have heavy clasps, which could weigh down a small puppy.

Collar

Select a collar that fits comfortably but not too loosely—two fingers should be able to fit between the collar and your puppy's neck. A collar that's too big could cause him to get caught, which could lead to panic or injury. Opt for quick-snap or buckle collars and avoid choke chains, prong collars, or electric collars.

It's also a good idea to get an ID tag for your puppy's collar. Choose a durable tag that won't tarnish or leave marks on his coat. Ensure it's the right size so it doesn't hang too far down. Alternatively, you can get a collar engraved with your contact information. Always make sure your puppy has identification on his collar, especially when leaving the house. If he escapes or gets lost, having identification gives him the best chance of returning home safely.

Harness

Certain dogs, especially those with flat faces (e.g., Pugs, Bulldogs), do better with a harness than a collar for walks. Harnesses are gentler on the airways and help prevent strain, particularly during walks or when pulling. Even if you don't have a brachycephalic dog, harnesses can still be useful.

Harnesses typically have two attachment points: one on the back near the shoulders and one on the front of the chest. A back-clip harness is humane and comfortable for your puppy but won't help much with pulling. If your puppy pulls a lot, consider a front-clip harness that redirects his movement and slows him down. Be sure the harness fits properly to avoid chafing or discomfort.

Head Halter

If you have a strong puppy or a larger breed, a head halter can be an effective training tool. Unlike choke chains, which put pressure on the trachea, head halters control the puppy's head. This gives you more control without causing harm or discomfort. A properly fitted head halter should not obstruct his breathing or cause pain.

Clicker

Clickers are small devices that emit a sharp sound, often used for clicker training. The sound is a great way to mark desired behaviors, and there are both loud and soft versions available. If you have difficulty pressing buttons, some clickers are easier to use, especially if you have arthritis. You can also get a wrist coil to keep the clicker easily accessible while training.

Crate

Crates are essential for house-training and keeping your puppy safe when unsupervised. A crate should be just big enough for your puppy to stand, turn around, and lie down comfortably. It teaches him to hold his bladder and bowels, as most puppies avoid soiling their "den."

Choose a sturdy crate—plastic or wire—depending on your needs. A plastic crate is easy to clean and some are airline-approved. Wire crates often fold for easy storage and include removable trays for cleaning. For larger puppies, consider getting a crate with a divider that adjusts as your puppy grows.

Toys

Toys are vital for your puppy's development, especially as they help with teething and discourage inappropriate chewing. Puppies enjoy chewing, and offering them appropriate chew toys will keep them from gnawing on your shoes or furniture.

There are many types of toys, and every puppy has different preferences. Some puppies may not show much interest in toys at first, but with encouragement, they can learn to play with them instead of chewing on things they shouldn't.

Chew Toys

When selecting chew toys, opt for durable ones that are larger than your puppy's mouth. This ensures that they cannot break into small pieces that could be swallowed, causing a choking hazard or internal injury. Some durable options include rubber toys, antlers, and marrow bones.

Interactive Toys

Interactive toys, such as treat-dispensing puzzles, provide both mental stimulation and entertainment. These toys challenge your puppy to work for their food, keeping them engaged and helping to prevent boredom. They are also great for crate time or when you need to leave your puppy unsupervised for a while.

Tug Toys

Tug-of-war is a fun, safe game for most puppies. Just ensure your puppy doesn't become too aggressive or possessive over the toy. Keep play sessions short to avoid excessive strain on their teeth and gums.

Balls

Balls are another popular toy, but make sure the ball is an appropriate size for your puppy's mouth. Tennis balls are fun, but ensure they aren't used as chew toys since their rough surface can wear down their teeth.

Flirt Pole

A flirt pole is a great exercise tool for energetic puppies. It's like a fishing pole with a toy attached to the end, and you can move it around to engage your puppy in chasing games. This is especially beneficial for breeds that love to chase or need a lot of physical activity.

Squeaky and Stuffed Toys

Many puppies love squeaky toys and stuffed animals, but ensure these are designed specifically for dogs. Be cautious with toys that have small parts like squeakers, as puppies can chew them out and swallow them. If you have children with stuffed animals, avoid giving your puppy those toys to prevent confusion.

Playing Games with Your Puppy

Playing with your puppy not only reinforces positive chewing behaviors but also teaches him how to interact with you. Teach your puppy to share his toys by playing with him, then allowing him some solo time with them. This helps him learn to amuse himself and fosters independence.

Start with simple games like hide-and-seek. Hide behind a corner, call your puppy, and reward him when he finds you. This will build a positive association with coming to you.

Exercise for a Healthy, Happy Puppy

Puppies are energetic one moment and napping the next. As they grow, their energy levels may seem boundless. Adequate exercise is essential for your puppy's physical and mental health, and it plays a key role in successful training.

Lack of exercise can lead to distracted, hyperactive behavior during training. If your puppy hasn't had enough exercise, he may have difficulty focusing or may act out during sessions. Exercise before training can help "calm the edge" and make your puppy more receptive to learning.

The amount of exercise your puppy needs depends on his age, breed, and individual energy levels. Sporting breeds will need more exercise than smaller companion dogs. As your puppy matures, his exercise needs will increase. Keep in mind his breed's history— some dogs were bred for high-energy tasks, and they may need activities to burn off that energy, even if you don't plan on engaging in those specific activities with them.

While walking is a great way to exercise your puppy, it may not be enough as he grows. Puppies often need more intense physical activity to burn off excess energy. A balance of walks, play, and other forms of exercise will keep your puppy fit and focused during training sessions.

Exercise and Weather Conditions

Weather plays a significant role in deciding whether your puppy can exercise or play outside. Some puppies are picky and refuse to go out in the rain, while others love splashing in puddles. Some enjoy playing in the snow, while others believe it's too dangerous. It's important to assess whether the outdoor temperature is safe for your puppy and to monitor them closely when outside to ensure their well-being.

In hot climates, be cautious of overheating. Signs of heatstroke in dogs include:

- Excessive panting
- Thick, sticky drool
- A bright red tongue
- Vomiting
- Diarrhea
- Dizziness

If you notice these symptoms, immediately remove your puppy from the heat and contact your vet or an emergency clinic.

Additionally, hot pavement can burn your puppy's paws. Since dogs don't wear shoes, walking on hot asphalt can cause pain or blisters. If you're in an area with sidewalks or grass, these are safer alternatives for your puppy. However, if you must walk on the street, be aware that asphalt can become dangerously hot. If your puppy starts "dancing" or seems distressed, check their paws for burns or blisters.

On the flip side, cold climates require their own precautions. Dogs, especially small breeds, those with short coats, and puppies, can be vulnerable to hypothermia, where the body temperature drops too low. Symptoms of hypothermia include:

- Lethargy
- Shivering
- Weak pulse
- Coma

If your puppy shows signs of hypothermia, bring them inside, wrap them in a blanket, and immediately call your vet or emergency clinic.

Frostbite, which can occur alongside hypothermia, usually affects the tail, ears, or paws. Areas affected by frostbite will appear pale, blue, or white. As circulation returns, the skin may turn bright red and peel. Over time, it may become black and extremely painful. If you suspect frostbite, gently warm the affected areas with lukewarm—not hot—water and contact your vet.

The Key to Effective Puppy Training: You

You play a crucial role in your puppy's training and development, which is a big responsibility! Be patient with both your puppy and yourself. Training takes effort, and you're bound to make some mistakes, especially if this is your first time training a dog. However, you can do it. Your puppy may test your patience, but remember, they are still a baby, and it's your job to teach them in ways they can understand.

Avoid using harsh tones when training. If you were in school and your teacher yelled all their instructions, it would have been stressful and unproductive. Likewise, you don't need to yell at your puppy to teach them. Reserve a firm tone for when they're doing something truly inappropriate (better yet, teach them not to do those things).

Use a friendly, calm voice during training. It's important not to associate your puppy's name or recall command with negative situations. Yelling "FIDO! COME HERE!" when angry will only teach them to avoid coming when you call. You don't want them to learn that!

Establish clear boundaries for acceptable behaviors, and make sure everyone in the household follows the same rules. For example, if you don't want your dog on the bed, don't let your new puppy sleep on the bed just because they're stressed in their first few days at home. It will only confuse and stress them out to change the rules once they're used to it.

Similarly, if you don't want your dog jumping on you when they're older, don't allow it as a puppy. It's tempting to let your adorable puppy jump up for kisses, but rewarding that behavior makes it harder to correct later. If you let it happen for a while and then suddenly try to stop it, your puppy will be confused.

It's best to set clear limits from the start and ease them as your puppy matures and learns control. For example, if you're okay with your dog jumping on you but you have small children or elderly people in your home, it's wise to train your puppy not to jump on people right from the start. Later, you can teach them a cue that allows them to jump up only when given permission, giving you control over when and to whom they jump.

The same approach applies to allowing your puppy on furniture. While you may not mind a grown dog lounging on the couch, teaching a puppy to jump up on it could result in messes or accidents. Start by teaching your puppy not to get on the furniture, and as they get older, you can introduce a cue that allows them to join you on the couch under your terms. This gives you control over when and how they access furniture.

Chapter 6: House-Training Your Puppy

House-training a puppy can be a frustrating experience for many pet owners. Cleaning up accidents is never enjoyable, and at times, it might feel as though your puppy is deliberately making messes to annoy you. However, it's important to understand that puppies don't eliminate out of spite. Pottying is a natural behavior for them, and they simply don't yet grasp that they shouldn't eliminate inside the house. Even if you think you've been clear about where you want them to go, they might not fully understand.

House-training requires consistency, patience, and clear communication. It also means you need to keep a very close eye on your puppy. The phrase "supervise your puppy" essentially means you should be vigilant, watching them closely to prevent accidents. Puppies can pee in an instant, and if you look away for just a few minutes, you may turn around to find a puddle on the floor.

Your puppy only eliminates in inappropriate places because you've allowed it. This usually happens because the puppy has too much freedom, not enough supervision, or you haven't taken them to their designated elimination area often enough. Every time your puppy goes potty in the wrong place, they're reinforcing that behavior. Your goal is to limit their chances to eliminate in places you don't want and make sure they have plenty of opportunities to eliminate where you do.

The first decision in house-training is where you want your puppy to go potty: indoors or outdoors? Pick one option to avoid confusing your puppy. If you want them to go outside sometimes and use pads inside at other times, it will only confuse them. Keep things straightforward.

If you choose outdoor elimination, your puppy will be trained to potty outside only. If you prefer indoor elimination, your puppy will be taught to use pads or a litter box. For example, if you want your puppy to eliminate outdoors, you shouldn't encourage them to use pads indoors as well.

Once you've decided on the elimination method, it's time to start confinement training, and a crate is an ideal tool for this.

Crate Training

A crate is a highly effective tool for house-training your puppy. When used properly, it teaches your puppy to hold their bladder and bowels because most puppies do not want to soil their sleeping area. Aside from house-training, crate training offers several other benefits:

- Crates keep your puppy safe from chewing harmful objects like electrical cords or small items they might swallow.
- Crates prevent destructive chewing on furniture, shoes, and household items, saving you from frustration.
- Crates help your puppy learn to be comfortable alone. Since you can't be with your puppy all the time, it's essential for them to get used to being alone in a safe space.
- Crates can aid in recovery after illness, injury, or surgery. For example, if your puppy has been spayed or neutered, they will need rest, and a crate will limit their activity.
- Crates are also great for travel. If your car is large enough, you can use the crate to keep your puppy safe during car

rides, preventing them from becoming a projectile in the event of an accident.

Using a crate for house-training is often more effective than confining your puppy to a room like the kitchen or bathroom. In a room, your puppy may just find a corner to eliminate and move away, but in a crate, they learn to hold their bladder and bowels more effectively.

If introduced properly, a crate can become your puppy's safe haven—a comforting den where they can rest when feeling tired or stressed. Many puppies will willingly go into their crate for naps once they become accustomed to it.

Crate Location

Where should you place your puppy's crate? Ideally, it should be in an area where you spend a lot of time, such as the living room or family room. If you want to move the crate into your bedroom at night, that's fine. In fact, it may help your puppy feel more secure being close to you.

Avoid placing the crate in a location where you don't spend much time, such as a laundry room. Puppies are social animals and want to be part of the family. Keeping the crate in a central location will help your puppy bond with you.

Crate Accessories

Puppies should always have access to water in their crate. Avoid plastic bowls that they could chew on; instead, opt for stainless steel bowls or "coop cups" that attach to the crate door. If your puppy is prone to spilling water, ensure they have plenty of access to water when out of the crate.

You can place a mat or blanket in the crate, but be aware that some puppies may chew on it. If this happens, remove the blanket to prevent your puppy from swallowing pieces. If your puppy is not a chewer, it's fine to leave the blanket in the crate.

A crate cover can also help provide a more den-like atmosphere for your puppy. However, if your puppy is a chewer, it's best to leave the crate uncovered to prevent them from pulling the fabric into the crate and chewing on it.

Do not use pee pads in the crate. Some pads are scented to encourage puppies to eliminate, which could teach your puppy to potty in the crate. Crate training is meant to teach your puppy to hold their bladder, not to go potty in their den. If you want to use pads for indoor elimination, that's fine, but avoid using them in the crate.

Introducing the Crate

The crate should always be a positive experience for your puppy. Never use it as a form of punishment.

Here's how to introduce your puppy to the crate:

1. Take your puppy to the crate and click and treat for any interest in the crate, even if they just look at it. Don't lure them into the crate with treats; let them explore on their own.
2. As your puppy begins to show more interest, click and treat when they interact with the crate.
3. Once your puppy puts a paw inside the crate, click and treat.

4. Wait for your puppy to put two paws inside the crate before clicking and treating.
5. Progress until your puppy goes fully into the crate, rewarding them with treats each time.

Once your puppy is reliably going into the crate, it's time to add a cue, such as "Kennel up" or "Go to crate." Say the cue just before your puppy enters, and reward them when they do.

Next, shut the crate door and reward your puppy with a treat through the door. Open the door and let them out if they want. Gradually increase the time the door stays closed as your puppy becomes more comfortable inside.

When your puppy can stay quietly in the crate for short periods with the door closed, start leaving the room for a few seconds at a time, rewarding them for staying calm. Gradually increase the duration you're away.

To help your puppy enjoy crate time even more, you can provide a food-stuffed rubber toy or chew bone when you're gone.

Tips for Crate Training Success:

- Don't let your puppy out of the crate if they're whining or barking. This only teaches them that noise will lead to freedom.
- Be consistent and patient—crate training can take several days, but your puppy will learn to love their crate as a safe space.

If you haven't finished crate training by the time you need to crate your puppy overnight, don't worry. Place your puppy in the crate with some treats and a toy, and leave them there overnight. If your puppy protests, check that they're not stuck or injured, but don't let them out until they're quiet. If the crate is in your bedroom, you can comfort them by letting them sniff your fingers through the door.

Remember, young puppies (around 8 weeks old) may need a potty break in the middle of the night. Take them outside and return them to the crate with a treat afterward.

When you're at home, allow your puppy to spend time outside the crate as long as you're supervising. Crate them occasionally even when you're home so they don't associate the crate with only your departure.

With patience and consistency, crate training will help your puppy feel secure in their space, and you'll both enjoy peaceful nights and stress-free days.

Establishing Schedules for Your Puppy

To ensure your puppy's success in house training, it's crucial to set regular feeding and potty schedules. Free feeding is generally not recommended as it can lead to irregular potty habits, making house training more challenging. If a puppy eats all day, he will also need to eliminate at various times throughout the day, complicating the process of teaching him where and when to go.

For puppies under six months old, it's ideal to provide three meals a day. Put the food down for about 15 minutes, and then take the bowl away, even if some food remains. This approach will help your puppy understand mealtime routines. He may even start reminding you when it's time to eat!

Try to space out meals evenly throughout the day. Avoid feeding your puppy too late in the evening, as this could lead to nighttime potty breaks. It's also a good idea to remove his water an hour before bedtime to help reduce nighttime potty trips. Just make sure he has plenty of water during the day.

Consistency is key, even on weekends. Puppies thrive on routine, so try to stick to the same schedule every day to help your puppy learn faster.

Your puppy's potty schedule will vary depending on his age and breed. Younger puppies (around 8-16 weeks old) need more frequent potty breaks than older puppies, and smaller breeds often require more breaks. In general, puppies need to eliminate after they wake up (from naps or sleep), after eating, after playing, and after baths. A good rule of thumb is to take your puppy for a potty break every couple of hours, especially in the early stages.

As your puppy matures, the frequency of potty breaks will decrease. For example, adult dogs typically need about four breaks a day, but your puppy will eventually transition from needing eight breaks to just four. However, every dog is different, and your puppy may need more or fewer breaks.

While schedules help keep you consistent and efficient in training, puppies don't always stick to the schedule! Learn to recognize the signs that your puppy needs to go. Very young puppies might not give clear signals right away, but as they grow, they'll start showing signs like whining, sniffing the ground, or circling. If you spot these cues, immediately take him to his designated potty spot.

Training Your Puppy to Potty Outside

If you don't have a yard, or if you plan to travel with your puppy, you'll need to teach him to eliminate during walks and in different environments. Some dogs may develop preferences for specific surfaces (like grass), so it's important to teach your puppy to eliminate on various types of ground—such as grass, rocks, or pine straw—to avoid confusion while traveling.

Simply putting your puppy outside on a schedule won't teach him to eliminate. Puppies are easily distracted, and he may not understand that the purpose of going outside is to potty. Keep him focused by always taking him out on a leash.

When on a leash, you can guide him to a specific elimination spot, avoiding distractions. This is especially helpful for busy schedules, travel, or when monitoring his health. Leashing also encourages quick potty breaks, which is ideal for maintaining efficiency.

You'll need to go outside with your puppy to effectively house-train him. Stay present when he eliminates so you can immediately reward him. Once he's fully house-trained, you won't have to accompany him outside.

Goal: Your   puppy   will   eliminate   outside.
What You'll Need: Treats, plastic bags for cleanup, leash.

1. Hide the treats to avoid distracting your puppy.

2. Leash your puppy and take him to his designated potty spot. If you're teaching him to potty during a walk, don't walk too far before reaching the spot.
3. As soon as he starts to eliminate, say "Go potty" in a cheerful tone.
4. Praise and reward him immediately after he finishes.
5. Let your puppy play or walk for a few minutes after pottying.
6. Repeat these steps consistently for each potty break.

Tip: Remember, house-training is a gradual process. Don't be discouraged by setbacks. If your puppy has a week of success, don't assume he's fully trained. Each accident can set you back, so continue with the training program until you achieve lasting success.

Once your puppy reliably eliminates on leash, you can begin to wean him off the leash in a secure, fenced yard. Here's how:

1. Take your puppy outside with the leash, but let him drag it behind him. If he eliminates, praise and reward him.
2. Gradually allow your puppy to go to the elimination spot on his own.
3. Increase the distance you stay from the elimination spot over time, ensuring he can reliably eliminate on his own.

Tip: If you face setbacks, like your puppy getting distracted outside, go back to using the leash and supervising closely. Be patient and consistent—puppies have short attention spans and will improve with time.

Training Your Puppy to Eliminate Indoors

If you live in a high-rise apartment or have a small dog, teaching your puppy to eliminate indoors can be a practical solution. This is also helpful if you can't always get home for potty breaks or if you travel frequently.

Indoor elimination can be a good option for travel, such as when staying in a hotel or visiting family, but it may not always be convenient for visitors who don't want an indoor potty station. To start, decide whether you want to train your puppy to use a litter box or pee pads. Litter boxes for dogs are different from those for cats—avoid using cat litter, as it can be harmful to your puppy. If you plan to transition to outdoor potty training, sod or turf are good options for the indoor station.

Goal: Your puppy will eliminate indoors in a designated spot.
What You'll Need: Elimination station, treats.

1. Hide the treats to avoid distractions.
2. Take your puppy to the elimination spot and encourage him to eliminate. When he does, give the cue ("Go potty"), praise, and reward him.
3. If after 10 minutes your puppy hasn't eliminated, confine or supervise him for 15 minutes, then try again.
4. Repeat consistently until he learns to eliminate in the designated spot.

Once your puppy is reliably eliminating on cue, you can start teaching him to go to the spot on his own:

1. Lead your puppy to the elimination spot but stop just short of it. Let him finish the journey alone.
2. Gradually increase the distance between you and the spot until you can direct him to the spot from another room.

Tip: If your puppy misses the litter box or pad, go back to the point where he was successful and repeat that step for a week before trying again. Be patient as your puppy learns, and ensure the path to the elimination spot is clear of obstacles. Accidents are normal, so stay consistent with training.

Advanced Training for Your Puppy

Once your puppy is consistently eliminating in the designated area, you can start considering more advanced training techniques if you wish.

Dog Doors

Some pet owners believe that installing a dog door will automatically teach their puppy to eliminate outdoors. While some puppies instinctively know to go outside, not all of them do, and relying solely on a dog door for house-training is not advisable. Moreover, if you ever travel to a place without a dog door, your puppy might be confused.

Another issue with using a dog door, especially without supervision, is that your puppy might bring unwanted items inside, ranging from sticks to even live animals. Puppies are naturally curious, so they're prone to carrying things in, and they may also take your belongings outside.

If you already have an older dog in the household that uses a dog door, don't expect them to teach your new puppy to eliminate outside. Sometimes, puppies learn by following older dogs outdoors, but when the older dogs are no longer around, the puppy may begin eliminating indoors. It's important to take an active role in teaching your puppy the right behavior.

Once your puppy has successfully house-trained for several months, you can start introducing them to the dog door.

Goal:

Teach your puppy to go through the dog door.

What You'll Need:
Clicker, treats.

Steps:

1. Sit near the dog door with your puppy. Click and treat for any interest in the door, even if they just look at it.
2. After a few clicks for showing interest, your puppy should start moving towards the door or nudging it with their nose. Click and treat. Gradually encourage your puppy to open the door with their nose. Click and treat for every successful attempt.
3. If your puppy seems hesitant or confused, open the door yourself and hold it open. Be sure it doesn't slam shut, as this could startle them. Click and treat for any exploratory behavior.
4. Gradually work towards getting your puppy to go through the dog door. Click and treat for every correct response.

5. Go outside through the dog door and repeat the process. Just because your puppy learns to go through the door one way doesn't mean they will automatically understand that they can come back through it.

Tip:
The process might take one session or several, depending on your puppy. Some puppies will confidently go through the door right away, while others may be more cautious. Go at your puppy's pace and celebrate their successes.

Teaching Your Puppy to Ring a Bell

As your puppy's house-training progresses, you can teach them to ring a bell to signal when they need to go outside to eliminate. This is ideal for puppies trained to eliminate exclusively outdoors.

Goal:
Teach your puppy to ring a bell when they need to go outside.

What You'll Need:
A bell attached to a long ribbon, clicker, treats, leash. Position the bell at your puppy's shoulder height so they can easily reach it with their paw. Attach the bell to the door you use to take your puppy outside for potty breaks.

Steps:

1. Sit near the bell and click and treat for any interest your puppy shows in it, even if they just look at it. As your puppy becomes more interested, they will start to nose or paw at the bell. Click and treat for these actions.

2. Once your puppy is consistently ringing the bell, it's time to associate ringing the bell with you opening the door. Leash your puppy and wait by the door for them to ring the bell. When they do, click, treat, and immediately open the door to take them outside. Give them a cue to eliminate and reward them afterward.
3. With repeated practice, your puppy will learn that ringing the bell means you'll open the door. Eventually, your puppy will ring the bell even when you're not near the door. If this happens, stop what you're doing, go to your puppy, leash them, and open the door. At this point, clicking isn't necessary anymore, as your puppy has already learned the behavior.
4. Allow your puppy 10 minutes to eliminate outside. If they do, praise and treat them. If not, bring them back inside. Your puppy may not yet understand that ringing the bell is only for when they need to eliminate, so be vigilant in ensuring they don't ring the bell just to go out and play.
5. Repeat this process each time your puppy rings the bell. It's common for puppies to ring it a lot at first, so be patient.

Tips:

If you suspect your puppy just wants to go outside to play, don't open the door. This could confuse them and disrupt your training. Even if they seem playful, go ahead and open the door to teach them that ringing the bell is reserved for potty time. By using a leash, you can prevent them from running off and help reinforce the connection between the bell and elimination.

Cleaning Up Messes

Even with the best training efforts, there will be times when your puppy eliminates in the wrong place. This is normal. Your goal is to minimize these accidents, but when they do happen, don't overreact.

If you catch your puppy in the act, firmly say "No!" and immediately take them to the designated elimination area (use a leash if you're training them to eliminate outside). Praise them enthusiastically if they finish in the correct spot.

Avoid using harsh punishment like hitting with your hands or a rolled-up newspaper. This can cause fear and confusion, and it won't teach your puppy to stop eliminating indoors. Instead, it might make them hide or eliminate in secret, which you want to avoid.

If you don't catch your puppy in the act, it's too late to punish them. Just focus on being more vigilant and prevent future accidents through increased supervision.

Chapter 7: Everyday Manners and Life Skills

As a puppy owner, it's your duty to ensure that your puppy behaves appropriately in public. Puppies are like babies, and they don't yet understand social norms. While you'll be teaching your puppy good manners, you'll also need to manage their behavior to prevent them from becoming a nuisance or accidentally causing harm to others, whether human or animal.

Setting Expectations

There are certain behaviors that are expected of well-mannered dogs in public. These include:

- **Leash Etiquette:** Puppies should always be leashed in public places where required. Allowing them to roam freely in neighborhoods can lead to accidents, such as being hit by cars, attacked by other dogs, or entering people's yards uninvited.
- **Respecting Other Dogs' Space:** Your puppy shouldn't approach another dog without the owner's consent. While it's great if your puppy is friendly and social, not all dogs appreciate an enthusiastic greeting. Unwanted interactions can lead to your puppy being bitten or scaring off a timid dog.
- **No Jumping on People:** While jumping is often a sign of excitement and friendliness in puppies, not everyone enjoys being jumped on. Depending on your puppy's size, they may even cause unintentional harm or discomfort.

- **Poop Responsibility:** It's your responsibility as a dog owner to clean up after your puppy. If they relieve themselves outside your property, make sure to pick up after them.

By simply keeping your puppy leashed in public or when guests are present, you can avoid most behavioral issues. As your puppy matures and learns good manners, managing their behavior will become easier.

The Collar and Leash: A Lifeline

Puppies aren't instinctively fond of collars or being controlled by a leash. Initially, they may scratch at their collars or resist walking with a leash. It's essential to help them associate these tools with positive experiences, like walks and playtime.

Goal: Help your puppy become comfortable with wearing a collar or harness.

What You Need: Collar, treats, toys.

Steps:

1. Let your puppy sniff the collar, and reward them with a treat. Repeat this several times.
2. Put the collar on your puppy, immediately giving them three treats. If they don't paw at the collar, remove it. Repeat this a few times.
3. Once your puppy is used to the collar, allow them to wear it for a few seconds and then remove it. Gradually increase the duration they wear it.

4. Praise your puppy and play with them while they wear the collar. Remove it quietly without drawing attention to it. The goal is to make the collar a positive experience.

Tips: If your puppy paws at the collar, don't remove it right away. Instead, distract them with a toy. Make sure the collar fits properly, as puppies grow quickly and can outgrow their collars.

Once your puppy is comfortable with their collar, you can begin leash training.

Goal: Your puppy will become accustomed to walking on a leash attached to their collar or harness.

What You Need: Leash, collar, treats.

Steps:

1. Attach the leash to your puppy's collar and reward them with treats.
2. Allow your puppy to drag the leash around in a safe space, ensuring it doesn't get tangled.
3. Hold the leash gently and offer treats as you practice.
4. Begin walking and encourage your puppy to follow. If they stop, don't force them—just wait until they start walking again. Offer praise and treats when they comply.
5. Repeat this process until your puppy comfortably follows your lead with gentle leash pressure.

Teaching Self-Control: "Settle Down"

Puppies can be incredibly energetic and may struggle with self-control. Teaching them to calm down on command is an important skill.

Goal: Your puppy will learn to settle and remain calm.

What You Need: Clicker, treats.

Steps:

1. Get your puppy excited by jumping, clapping, or using a high-pitched voice. Once they're riled up, stop all movement and remain still. Wait for them to calm down. Once they do, reward them with a click and a treat.
2. Repeat the process several times.
3. Add a cue word like "Calm" or "Settle" right before you stop moving. Reward your puppy for settling down after the cue.
4. Gradually reduce the frequency of treats as your puppy becomes more consistent in responding to the cue.

Bite Inhibition

Puppies naturally chew as part of exploring their environment and teething. However, they need to learn that biting humans is not acceptable.

Goal: Your puppy will learn bite inhibition and stop mouthing you.

What You Need: Toys.

Steps:

1. When your puppy's teeth make contact with your skin, let out a loud "ow!" to simulate pain. Don't yell or sound angry, as this might encourage them to bite harder.
2. Withdraw your attention completely. Puppies often stop chewing when they realize they've caused discomfort.
3. Offer a toy to redirect their chewing. Praise them when they chew on the toy instead of you.
4. Be consistent—repeat this every time your puppy mouths you.

Avoid roughhousing with your puppy, as it can encourage mouthing behavior. If you don't want them to bite, never encourage or play games that involve biting.

Trade Exercises to Prevent Resource Guarding

Resource guarding occurs when a dog tries to protect an object they perceive as valuable, such as a toy or food. To prevent this, teach your puppy to relinquish items willingly.

Goal: Your puppy will learn to give up items when cued.

What You Need: Two items that your puppy likes.

Steps:

1. Give your puppy a toy and let them chew on it for a few minutes.
2. Offer them a second toy and, when they take it, praise them. Pick up the first toy.
3. Repeat several times and end the session.

Tip: Vary the items you use to keep the exercise engaging.

Handling: Teaching Comfort with Touch

Your puppy should be comfortable being touched all over their body, including their ears, paws, mouth, and tail. This is important for future grooming, veterinary visits, and general care.

Goal: Your puppy will learn to enjoy being handled.

What You Need: Treats.

Steps:

1. Gently touch your puppy's ears, and immediately give them a treat. Do this for both ears.
2. Touch each of their paws lightly and reward them with treats.
3. Gently open your puppy's mouth, and give a treat.
4. Touch their tail lightly, and reward with a treat.
5. Repeat all steps several times, ensuring that each touch is followed by a reward.

As your puppy becomes more comfortable with handling, progress to gently massaging their ears, paws, mouth, and tail.

Tips: Some puppies may be more sensitive about certain areas, like their mouths. Be patient and use high-value treats to reward progress. Slow down if your puppy seems uncomfortable, and gradually build up to full handling.

Nail Clipping

Once your puppy is comfortable being touched, you can start introducing them to nail clipping.

Goal: Your puppy will become comfortable with nail clipping.

What You Need: Nail clippers, treats, styptic powder.

Steps:

1. Show your puppy the nail clippers and reward them with a treat.
2. Repeat this step several times over the course of a week.
3. Touch a nail with the clippers (without cutting), and reward with a treat.
4. Once your puppy is comfortable, cut one nail, reward with treats, and stop the session.
5. Gradually increase the number of nails you clip over several sessions.

Tip: Go slowly and ensure your puppy is comfortable throughout the process. Don't rush it, as forcing the experience could cause setbacks in training.

Chapter 8: Socialization

There is some debate over the exact age when a puppy's socialization window closes, typically between twelve and eighteen weeks. However, there is no debate about how critical this period is. During this time, puppies learn about the world around them and form lasting impressions that influence their behavior as adults.

If a puppy doesn't experience positive exposure to a variety of people, animals, environments, surfaces, sounds, and other stimuli during this period, it may develop fears of these things later in life. For instance, if a puppy hasn't interacted with children and encounters a toddler at a year old, it might growl at the child. Toddlers behave differently from adults—they move unpredictably, make loud noises, and grab things abruptly, which can be startling to an unaccustomed puppy. On the other hand, a puppy that has been positively exposed to children before the age of eighteen weeks is more likely to feel comfortable around them as an adult.

When people adopt a rescue dog that exhibits fear toward certain groups, like men, children, or specific situations, they often assume it's due to previous abuse. While abuse is a possibility, it is not the primary cause in every case. More often, it's because the dog didn't receive proper socialization during its critical developmental period.

For example, if a puppy was mostly raised in a backyard with other dogs and had little interaction with people, it is likely to bond well with dogs but remain wary of humans. This happens because the puppy missed the chance to socialize with people during that critical period. Many rescue dogs exhibit this pattern—they interact well with other dogs but are fearful of people, due to insufficient human exposure as puppies.

The socialization period is one of the most important stages of your puppy's life, and you bear a significant responsibility to get it right. Neglecting this crucial period can result in serious behavioral issues later. To stay on track, use a calendar to track how much time remains until your puppy's socialization window closes. Commit to regular outings each week, introducing your puppy to different places, people, and animals, and make this your puppy's social calendar. Having set "appointments" will help you plan and maintain consistency.

However, socialization isn't just about taking your puppy everywhere. It's important to ensure that each new experience is a positive one. Watch for signs of fear or stress, and if a situation becomes overwhelming, ease off. Negative experiences can leave a lasting impact and may lead to the very behaviors you're trying to avoid.

Recognizing Signs of Fear and Helping Your Puppy Cope

As you socialize your puppy, it's essential to watch for signs of stress. Many pet owners fail to notice when their puppies are afraid. Familiarize yourself with the signs of distress, which include:

- Licking lips
- Yawning
- Turning away
- Tucking the tail
- Trying to avoid the situation

- Refusing treats

If your puppy shows any of these signs, assess the situation carefully. What is causing the stress? Try to create some distance or reduce the intensity of the situation to make it less frightening. Use positive reinforcement by clicking and rewarding calm behavior.

For example, if your puppy is frightened by a tall man wearing a hat, ask the man to sit down so he doesn't seem as imposing. Move your puppy away from the man and reward him for any brave actions, like looking toward the man. Encourage gradual interaction, with your friend slowly offering treats as the puppy becomes more comfortable.

If you're not making progress, it's better to remove your puppy from the situation than to force him to confront his fear. Forcing a puppy to face something that scares him can damage the trust between you and him. For instance, allowing a scared puppy to be picked up by a tall, unfamiliar man will only increase his fear.

Some owners mistakenly interpret their puppy's frantic licking as affection, but it's often an appeasement behavior. The puppy is trying to calm himself, not show affection. It's essential to consider the entire body language context.

Even the most confident puppies can be startled by unexpected things. A bouncy puppy might be scared of the vacuum cleaner or an umbrella. By being prepared and observant, you can help your puppy overcome these fears in a positive way.

Socializing Safely

While socialization is crucial, you must also be mindful of your puppy's health. During the socialization window, your puppy hasn't completed his vaccination series, including the rabies shot. This means you should avoid places where infected dogs might have been, such as pet stores, public parks, and your neighborhood, where diseases like distemper and parvovirus can spread through bodily fluids.

To keep your puppy safe, avoid these areas unless you can carry him, especially if he is small enough. Larger puppies are harder to carry but can still be safely socialized with a little creativity. Instead of taking your puppy to potentially risky places, bring experiences to him. Invite people and vaccinated dogs to visit you. Take your puppy to dog-friendly stores where he can ride in a shopping cart, keeping the experience positive. If you visit a friend's yard, ensure it hasn't been exposed to contagious diseases like parvovirus, which can survive for months in the environment.

If your puppy does need to walk in areas where disease is a concern, carry wipes to clean his paws afterward. Also, ensure that visitors wash their hands before interacting with your puppy, especially if they've been in potentially contaminated areas.

By taking these precautions, the benefits of socializing your puppy will far outweigh the risks. Proper socialization prevents future behavioral problems, such as fear and aggression.

Meeting New People

Dr. Ian Dunbar, a renowned veterinarian and behaviorist, recommends that puppies meet at least one hundred people during their socialization period. Aim to expose your puppy to a wide range of individuals, including people of different ages, genders, and ethnicities. It's important that these individuals are comfortable and confident with puppies; otherwise, the puppy may pick up on their nervousness, which could cause fear.

Encourage people to offer treats to your puppy in an open hand to avoid accidental nips from those sharp puppy teeth. While introducing your puppy to different people, observe his reactions— does he seem more hesitant around certain types of people? If so, give those individuals special treats to encourage positive associations.

Meeting Children

When socializing your puppy with children, choose kids who are gentle and can follow your instructions. Avoid introducing your puppy to children who are afraid of dogs, as this could create fear in your puppy as well. If your puppy is in a nippy phase, have the children drop treats on the floor rather than offering them directly to the puppy, especially if the puppy is teething.

Children often love picking up puppies, but this can be a poor socialization experience unless they know how to handle the puppy correctly. Only allow children to pick up the puppy if they can do so gently and supportively, ensuring the puppy feels secure. Never let children lift a puppy by the front legs or carry them like a toy, as this could cause distress.

Meeting Other Dogs

Before allowing your puppy to meet another dog, make sure the other dog is well-behaved and comfortable around puppies. Not all dogs get along with puppies, and even those that do may be too energetic for safe play. Always check with the other dog's owner to ensure the dog's temperament is suitable for interacting with your puppy.

If the interaction will be safe, it's often best to let the dogs meet off-leash in a fenced area, as leash tension can lead to aggression. Stay close by to intervene if necessary. If the dogs need to be on-leash, keep the leashes relaxed to reduce tension, but not so loose that they might become tangled. Short, controlled introductions are best, and you should allow the dogs to interact for brief periods, gradually increasing the time as they become more comfortable with each other.

Be attentive to the dogs' behavior during play. Canine play should be mutual and enjoyable for both dogs. It's normal for dogs to switch roles during play, but if either dog seems stressed or uncomfortable, remove them from the situation.

If you already have other dogs at home, the same introduction principles apply. Monitor the interactions closely to ensure everyone is getting along. Older dogs may need breaks from a lively puppy, and vice versa.

Even if your puppy interacts with other dogs at home, make sure he meets a variety of dogs outside your household to ensure he's well-socialized with different breeds and personalities.

Socialization Games

Socializing your puppy may seem like hard work, but it doesn't have to be dull! Socialization games can make the process fun for both you and your puppy, helping to ensure that he enjoys meeting new people, dogs, and experiences. Here are some fun games to incorporate into your socialization routine.

Handling Games

You can invite friends or family members to participate in the handling training exercise with your puppy. Make sure to select people who are comfortable around puppies and know how to handle them gently—no grabbing! This is an excellent opportunity for your puppy to get used to being touched by different people, as your veterinarian and groomer will also need to handle him. The exercise will be more effective if your puppy is calm beforehand, so play with him, let him run around, or do another activity to burn off some energy before starting the game.

To prepare, take one meal's worth of your puppy's kibble and divide it into separate baggies for each participant. Add a few extra tasty treats to each bag. As each person gently touches your puppy's paws, ears, mouth, or tail, they will give him a treat as positive reinforcement.

Tip: If your puppy becomes too squirmy or starts nipping at people's hands, he may need a break. He could be overwhelmed, so try tiring him out more and give it another go later.

Scavenger Hunts

Create a scavenger hunt to incorporate fun socialization exercises for your puppy. Throughout the hunt, your puppy will receive lots of treats, and you should reward yourself too for completing it! For example, during one outing, aim to:

1. Meet a stranger wearing a hat or hoodie.
2. Meet a small group of children.
3. Meet a man with a beard.
4. Meet two people wearing sunglasses.
5. Meet someone using a cane or crutches.
6. Meet a child on a skateboard.
7. See a balloon.
8. Experience a sudden noise.
9. Watch a sprinkler when it turns on.
10. See a big truck drive by.

Bring your clicker and treats. When your puppy shows brave, confident behavior, click and treat. If you're meeting people, they can reward your puppy with treats as well. If you're just observing from a distance, you can give the treats yourself.

Take note of your puppy's preferences and anxieties. If certain situations make him nervous, revisit those during the next scavenger hunt to help him build more positive associations.

Circle of Friends

This game involves a group of people, ideally enough to form a large circle while sitting on the ground. Prepare separate baggies of your puppy's kibble for each person, adding a few tasty treats to each one. Everyone should have a clicker.

Each person will take turns calling your puppy's name in a friendly voice, encouraging him to come over. When the puppy approaches, click and treat. Continue taking turns randomly around the circle. This game helps your puppy develop positive associations with approaching different people. Try varying the people in the circle each time so your puppy learns to approach a variety of individuals with confidence.

Doggy Daycare

Doggy daycare seems like a great option—your puppy gets to play with other dogs, stay socialized, and come home exhausted. However, not all daycare facilities are run by experienced professionals who understand canine behavior. Some daycares let puppies run loose with little supervision, which can be harmful to their development. If your puppy faces bullying or learns to be aggressive towards others, it could negatively impact his future interactions with dogs.

Before sending your puppy to daycare, do your research. Interview staff members about their experience in canine behavior. An answer like "I've had puppies all my life" isn't sufficient—ask them to explain how they recognize signs of stress, when they separate dogs, and how they handle inappropriate behavior. Do they use positive reinforcement methods?

Also, observe the daycare yourself. Check for cleanliness and ensure that dogs of different sizes are separated for safety. If you decide to try daycare, monitor your puppy's behavior afterward. If he shows signs of stress, such as shying away from other dogs or reacting aggressively, this could indicate that the daycare environment isn't ideal for his socialization.

A daycare might be a better option once your puppy has completed his early socialization period and has already formed positive associations with other dogs.

When the Window Closes, Open the Door

Socializing your puppy during his early weeks is essential, but once the "critical window" for socialization closes, that doesn't mean you should stop. While the early weeks are a time to be particularly intensive in socializing, it's important to continue the process through adolescence.

Puppies who receive early socialization but are not consistently exposed to new experiences later on may develop behavioral issues as adults. These can include fearfulness around certain types of people, places, or other dogs. To avoid this, keep up the socialization activities like scavenger hunts and meeting new people, even after your puppy's initial training period.

Once your puppy has received all his vaccinations, it will be easier (and safer) to take him to more places. This ongoing exposure will help him grow into a well-rounded, confident adult dog.

Chapter 9: Enrolling in Training Classes

While books and videos can teach you a lot about dog training, you may also want to consider enrolling your dog in a formal training class. Just like in any profession, there are both good and bad trainers, as well as high-quality and low-quality classes. It's important to take your time and choose a class that will provide a great experience for both you and your puppy. Before signing up, observe a class to get a feel for the trainer and the environment. A reputable instructor will be happy to let you do this.

What to Look for in a Trainer

When evaluating a trainer, consider their methods, experience, and qualifications.

Positive Training Methods

The trainer should use positive reinforcement techniques. While some websites or brochures may claim to use "positive methods," it's important to dig deeper. Look for trainers who use clicker training or lure-and-reward techniques. Avoid trainers who start with positive methods but then resort to corrections, such as collar yanks or physical punishment, once the dog is expected to "know better." Stay away from trainers who use choke chains, prong collars, or shock collars, as these are not necessary for training good behavior.

Experience and Education

The trainer should have substantial experience and formal education in canine behavior. Anyone can call themselves a dog trainer, as there is no certification or license required. Be sure to ask about their specific education. Simply saying "I've had dogs all my life" is not enough. Just because a trainer has earned titles with their own dogs does not necessarily mean they have the experience to train others or teach family manners. If you're interested in competitive events, look for a trainer with proven success in the field, but if you're just working on everyday behavior, this should not be a deciding factor.

Ask where the trainer was educated and whether they continue their education through conferences, workshops, or webinars. A quality trainer is always updating their knowledge. Avoid trainers who claim that their methods have always been successful without acknowledging the evolution of dog training. Dog training has come a long way, and staying updated is essential.

Certifications

Inquire whether the trainer holds any certifications. The Certification Council for Professional Dog Trainers (CCPDT) is the primary independent organization offering certification for dog trainers. Trainers who hold CCPDT certifications have completed a certain number of hours as a lead instructor, obtained recommendations from peers and clients, and passed a proctored exam. To maintain their certification, trainers must also continue their education. While other schools and programs may also offer credentials, make sure they align with modern, positive methods and require ongoing education.

While a trainer without certification may still be good, ask whether they are working toward credentials. Sometimes, certification may be too expensive for some trainers, but their commitment to using positive methods should be clear.

Professional Associations

Trainers who belong to professional organizations, such as the Association of Professional Dog Trainers (APDT) or the International Association of Animal Behavior Consultants (IAABC), often demonstrate a commitment to their craft. While membership doesn't guarantee quality, it shows that the trainer takes their profession seriously. Ask whether the trainer participates in the association, attends conferences, or stays updated on the latest research.

Evaluating the Class

When visiting a class, look for the following qualities:

- **Respectful Treatment**: Trainers and assistants should treat both dogs and people with respect. No one should feel singled out or bullied.
- **Positive Atmosphere**: The tone of the class should be upbeat and encouraging.
- **Open Communication**: The trainer should offer opportunities to ask questions, either during the class or afterward by phone or email.
- **Good Instructor-to-Student Ratio**: A ratio of about one trainer per eight students is ideal. If the class has one trainer for twenty students, it may be less effective unless there are qualified assistants present.
- **Enjoyment**: Both dogs and owners should be visibly enjoying the class.

Safety

The class should provide a safe environment for both dogs and owners, with enough space for each dog. If any dog shows reactivity, the trainer should quickly intervene. This doesn't mean punishing the dog; it may involve creating a barrier to prevent the reactive dog from seeing the other dogs or temporarily removing them from the class if necessary.

No Guarantees

A good trainer will not offer guarantees about your dog's behavior. While this may seem unusual, remember that dog training is not like purchasing an appliance. It would be unethical for a trainer to promise specific results because much of your dog's success depends on your commitment to continuing the training at home. The trainer can't control your environment or ensure that you follow through with the necessary work.

Additionally, the trainer should have business liability insurance for your peace of mind.

Training Clubs

Training clubs, often affiliated with organizations like the American Kennel Club (AKC), can also be an option for group classes. These clubs focus on competitive events where dogs earn ribbons and titles in agility, obedience, and rally. If you plan to pursue these activities, training clubs can be a good place to learn from experienced competitors. However, many trainers at these clubs are volunteers, so make sure they meet your standards and use modern, positive methods. You might want to enlist a professional trainer for initial lessons before joining a training club for further competitive development.

Private Lessons

Some people prefer private lessons to group classes. This could be due to scheduling conflicts, a preference for one-on-one instruction, or because their dog is too shy or reactive for a group setting. In such cases, it's important to apply the same criteria for selecting a trainer as you would for a group class.

Keep in mind that private lessons cannot be observed, so it's important to thoroughly vet the trainer before committing. Trainers who offer private lessons should provide a professional contract that outlines both their responsibilities and yours. Always read the contract carefully and keep a copy for your records.

Day Training and Board & Train Programs

Day training and board & train programs are options for those who prefer a trainer to do most of the work. These programs involve the trainer working with your dog either in your home (day training) or at the trainer's facility (board & train). However, many people mistakenly think that these programs mean the dog will be fully trained by the time it's returned. This is not true. You will need to attend transfer sessions where the trainer teaches you how to continue working with your dog, otherwise, your dog will only respond to the trainer and not to you.

When selecting a day training or board & train program, use the same criteria as you would for a private trainer. Be cautious of trainers who promise "boot camps" or quick fixes. Ask specific questions about the techniques they will use, how many dogs they work with at once, and what kind of environment your dog will be in. For board & train, ensure that your dog will have proper living conditions and care. Always ask for references and check them before committing.

Chapter 10: Basic Cues

Basic cues are essential foundation behaviors for any pet dog. Teaching these cues will improve your relationship with your dog and promote good manners. For instance, a dog that understands *Sit* is less likely to jump on people when greeting them. A dog that knows how to *Walk Nicely on Leash* won't pull you down the street. A dog that can hold a *Down-Stay* will calmly lie on its bed while you have guests over.

These basic cues also enhance your dog's safety. A dog that knows *Come* will return to you when called, preventing it from running off. A dog that understands *Leave It* will avoid dangerous objects or situations when instructed, which could save its life.

Additionally, these basic cues serve as the foundation for more advanced behaviors. For example, you begin teaching *Come* with your dog on a leash before progressing to an off-leash recall.

Have a Plan

Before you begin training, it's important to have a clear goal. Without one, you won't be able to focus your training effectively. Consider these steps:

- **What exactly will you teach?** Visualize what you want the behavior to look like.
- **What do you want to achieve in this session?** Some behaviors can be taught in one session, but many take several. Set a goal for this particular training session.

- **What will you do if you don't meet your goal?** If your dog is struggling, how will you adjust the session to keep it positive?
- **What if your dog exceeds your expectations?** Be prepared to move to the next step if your dog progresses quickly. Always have a plan for the next phase.

Before each session, ensure you have all necessary tools and treats on hand. Forgetting items like your clicker or treats can create confusion and frustration for your dog.

Keep training sessions short—just a few minutes at a time. Ending a session while your dog is succeeding ensures they remain motivated and excited for the next one. It's better to finish early than to push your dog too hard.

To help manage the length of sessions, consider training during TV commercials, or count out 10-20 treats. When the treats run out, it's time to stop.

Tracking Your Progress

Recording your dog's progress during training is a helpful tool. While keeping detailed charts can be tedious, even simple notes can be effective. Documenting your sessions can show you what's working and help identify any issues. This is especially useful when tackling difficult behaviors, or if multiple people are training your dog.

By noting what happens during each session, you can track improvements or setbacks. If you're teaching a dog to stop jumping on people, you might notice gradual progress. In one session, your dog might jump six out of ten times; in another, four out of ten. Even if the behavior isn't perfect yet, your notes will highlight the progress, helping you stay patient and focused.

If the behavior is worsening, it's a sign that adjustments are needed—perhaps you're adding distractions too soon, or your dog is not progressing as expected. If your dog starts showing signs of stress, like yawning or trying to walk away, this could indicate frustration or fatigue. Adjusting your training pace or revisiting a previous step can help resolve this.

If your dog shows signs of illness or injury, it's important to note these changes as well. This information can be helpful to your veterinarian if necessary.

Practice Makes Perfect

Consistency is key to successful dog training. Short, daily training sessions are more effective than long, repetitive ones that may bore both you and your dog. Aim for at least 15 minutes of training per day, breaking it into multiple short sessions. For puppies, keep sessions even shorter to avoid overwhelming them.

Adults may be able to handle longer sessions, but it's important to keep them engaging and productive. If you want to train for longer than 15 minutes, break it up into several short sessions.

When you decide to train can depend on the behavior you're working on. If your dog is excited when you return home from work, it's a good time to practice *Come*, but not *Sit-Stay*, as they might be too excited to focus. For behaviors like *Sit* or *Down*, practice after your dog has had some exercise and is a little calmer.

Teaching the Basic Lessons

Every dog is unique. A young, energetic dog might find stationary behaviors like *Sit-Stay* or *Down-Stay* more challenging than an older, calmer dog. However, a young dog might learn a fast *Recall* more easily.

Some breeds, such as active Golden Retrievers, may struggle with stationary cues, while others, like Mastiffs, might find them easier. Regardless of breed or age, all dogs can learn. It's never too late to teach an older dog new tricks, and it's a misconception that some breeds are unable to learn.

Watch Me

This behavior is designed to capture and maintain your dog's attention. When your dog is looking at you, they're less likely to focus on other distractions, like other dogs or animals. You can use this cue as a precursor to other commands, such as getting your dog to focus on you before you start walking him on a leash.

Goal: Your dog will make eye contact with you when you call his name.

What You'll Need: Clicker, treats, and optionally a leash (especially if your dog is easily distracted in quiet environments).

Preparation: Start training in a calm, quiet room with minimal distractions, removing any toys or items that might draw your dog's attention.

1. Stand still and wait for your dog to look you in the eyes.

2. As soon as your dog makes eye contact, click and treat. Ensure he's looking at you, not at your hand or the treats.
3. Repeat this process for ten repetitions, then end the session.
4. Continue practicing until your dog consistently makes eye contact.

Tip: Be patient—puppies may find this exercise challenging due to their heightened curiosity. If eye contact happens quickly, be ready to click!

Once your dog is reliably making eye contact, it's time to add the verbal cue.

1. Call your dog's name once, using a friendly tone, and wait for him to look at you.
2. As soon as he makes eye contact, click and treat.
3. Repeat for ten repetitions, then end the session.
4. Continue until your dog responds consistently to his name with eye contact in distraction-free environments.

Walking Nicely on Leash

Polite leash behavior is a common goal for dog owners. No one enjoys being dragged along the street, and it can be dangerous if you trip or strain yourself while walking a dog that's pulling hard.

Dogs don't pull to assert dominance—they simply want to explore. Their natural instinct is to move quickly, especially when there are interesting smells to discover. Pulling becomes a habit when dogs are rewarded for it (e.g., when they get closer to a smell or find something new by pulling on the leash).

Goal: Your dog will walk beside you without pulling, staying on one side and not cutting ahead or behind.

What You'll Need: Clicker, treats, leash, optional front-clip harness or head halter.

Preparation: Decide on which side you want your dog to walk. Being consistent is key. If you're planning on formal competition, use the left side, but otherwise, choose what feels best. Ensure everyone in the household works with the dog on the same side.

You'll also need to decide how to manage the leash, treats, and clicker. One setup could be to hold the leash in your right hand and treats in your left hand if your dog is on your left side.

Training Location: Begin in a quiet space with minimal distractions, such as inside your home or in your yard.

1. Put your dog on a leash and stand next to him, both facing the same direction.
2. Take two steps. Just before stopping, click and treat. Hold the treat near your side so your dog must stay by your side to receive the reward.
3. Repeat this sequence 19 more times, then end the session.
4. Continue practicing until your dog reliably stays next to you throughout the entire training session.

Tip: This exercise reinforces that staying close to you is more rewarding than pulling ahead. Keep the initial steps short to avoid allowing your dog to get ahead of you.

During real walks, continue to provide exercise, but practice this training separately. Dogs need time to focus on leash manners without the distractions of a walk or outdoor environment.

Once your dog is walking nicely by your side at two paces, you can gradually increase the challenge.

1. After the warm-up, take two steps and treat before stopping.
2. Repeat this until your dog remains by your side.
3. Gradually increase the number of steps before you click and treat.
4. Increase the challenge by walking through new environments with more distractions, such as around your house or outdoors.
5. If your dog gets distracted, click and treat more often to reinforce his position.

Tip: Always click before your dog pulls ahead. If he does, encourage him to return to your side to earn the reward.

Sit

This is a fundamental behavior that can help with various situations, like preventing your dog from bolting out the door or jumping on guests. A dog that knows "Sit" can't chase after things while in the sitting position.

Goal: Your dog will sit, placing his rear on the ground.

What You'll Need: Clicker, treats.

1. Hold a treat just above your dog's nose. Slowly move it upwards, leading his nose upward.
2. As your dog's rear touches the ground, click and toss a treat a couple of feet away to encourage him to get up and reset.
3. Repeat the steps two more times.
4. Now, without the treat in your hand, use the same hand motion as before. When your dog sits, click and toss a treat.
5. Repeat this five times, then end the session.

Tip: After the first three repetitions, stop using the treat in your hand to lure him. This prevents dependency on treats and teaches a hand signal for "Sit."

Once your dog reliably sits, it's time to add the verbal cue.

1. Cue "Sit" in a friendly tone, using the same hand motion.
2. When your dog sits, click and treat.
3. Repeat for ten repetitions, then end the session.

Down

Teaching your dog to lie down is valuable for settling him when you need him to stay calm, such as when visitors arrive.

Goal: Your dog will lie down.

What You'll Need: Clicker, treats.

Preparation: Teach "Sit" first.

1. Cue your dog to "Sit."

2. Hold a treat near your dog's nose, then move it downward under his chin and toward his chest.
3. Move the treat downward and between his front paws. Your dog's nose should follow the treat. If he raises his rear, reset him into a sit and start again, moving the treat more slowly.
4. Once your dog's belly touches the floor, click and toss a treat a few feet away to reset him.
5. Repeat the steps two more times.
6. Once he's consistently following the treat to the floor, perform the same motion with an empty hand. When your dog lies down, click and treat.
7. Repeat five times, then end the session.

Tip: Like "Sit," don't use a treat in your hand after the first three repetitions. Your dog will learn the motion without becoming dependent on the treat.

Once your dog reliably lies down, it's time to add the verbal cue.

1. Cue "Down" once in a friendly tone, using the same hand motion.
2. When your dog lies down, click and treat.
3. Repeat for ten repetitions, then end the session.

Recall Training: The "C ome" Command

Goal: To teach your dog to come when called, ensuring it's a positive and rewarding experience.

Why It's Important: Teaching your dog to come when called can be life-saving. If your dog ever escapes its collar while out on a walk, you want it to return to you promptly upon hearing your command.

Key Principle: Always make coming to you a pleasant experience for your dog. Never call your dog to you only to punish or scold it. This creates a negative association and will make your dog avoid you in the future. Avoid calling your dog for unpleasant situations like taking medicine or tending to an injury. In those cases, it's better to approach your dog with treats and make the experience positive.

Equipment Needed:

- Clicker
- Treats
- Leash

Preparation:

- Start by teaching your dog the **Hand Target** behavior.

Step-by-Step Training:

1. Start with Hand Targeting

- Attach a leash to your dog. Begin by cueing several "Touch" commands, asking your dog to touch its nose to your hand.
- Click and treat every correct response. Toss the treat behind your dog so it has to turn away to get it.
- Repeat this for a few repetitions to get your dog comfortable with targeting your hand.

2. Increasing the Distance

- Gradually toss the treat further behind your dog, prompting them to come back to you for the next repetition.
- Do this for 10 repetitions, ending the session afterward.

3. Introducing the Sit

- When your dog is reliably coming to touch your hand, introduce the "Sit" command.
- Cue "Touch," and when your dog touches your hand, click and toss the treat about 6 feet behind it.
- Before your dog reaches you, cue "Sit." When it sits, click and reward with a treat.
- Repeat this for 10 repetitions.

4. Adding the Final Cue

- Once your dog reliably comes to you and sits, replace the "Touch" cue with your final cue word (e.g., "Come!").
- Use "Come!" followed by "Touch," and when your dog sits, click and treat.
- Repeat this 8 times, then use just the "Come!" cue, clicking and treating every correct response.
- End the session after five repetitions.

5. Speeding Up the Recall

- Start walking with your dog on a leash and allow it to wander ahead.
- When your dog is ahead, call "Come!" and begin jogging backward.
- Stop after about 10 feet, allowing your dog to catch up and sit. Once it sits, click and toss the treat ahead of you.

- Repeat this for 10 repetitions, ending the session.
- *Tip: Be careful while jogging, and remember, the goal is to encourage your dog to run toward you.*

Sit-Stay Training

Goal: To teach your dog to hold a sit position for longer durations.

Why It's Useful: This command is essential if you plan to enter formal competitions or simply need your dog to stay still for pictures or while waiting.

Step-by-Step Training:

1. **Start with a Basic Sit**
   - Cue your dog to "Sit."
   - Wait for 3 seconds, then click and treat. Toss the treat so your dog has to stand up and reset for the next repetition.
   - Gradually increase the waiting time to 5, 8, and 2 seconds.
   - Repeat this 6 times, varying the length of time for which you ask your dog to hold the position. Aim for a 10-second hold before ending the session.
2. **Varying the Duration**
   - After your dog is reliably sitting for 10 seconds, you'll gradually build duration and distance.
   - Reward your dog intermittently during the duration (not just at the end) to encourage them to stay in place longer.
3. **Building Duration:**
   - Cue "Sit." Wait for 10 seconds, then reward.

- Then wait for 5 seconds and reward.
- Gradually increase and vary the waiting time to keep your dog engaged.
- Aim to work up to a longer hold time before rewarding.

Adding Distance to Sit-Stay:

1. Cue "Sit."
2. Step away from your dog by 2 steps, then return immediately to reward.
3. Gradually increase the number of steps you take away from your dog.
4. Don't always increase the distance in each session. Sometimes, step back just 2 steps for some repetitions to keep your dog from becoming too distracted.
5. End the session when your dog is doing well.

Down-Stay Training

Goal: To teach your dog to hold a down position for longer durations.

Step-by-Step Training:

1. **Start with Down**
   - Cue "Down."
   - Wait 3, 5, 8, and 2 seconds, rewarding with a treat each time.
   - Increase the time gradually to 10 seconds.
2. **Building Duration:**

- After your dog is reliably lying down for 10 seconds, increase the duration over time.
- Use similar techniques as you did for the Sit-Stay to help your dog stay longer.

3. **Adding Distance to Down-Stay:**
   - Start by cueing your dog to "Down."
   - Take a few steps away, returning immediately to reward your dog.
   - Gradually increase the number of steps, ensuring you always return to reward your dog.

4. **Vary the Distance:**
   - Mix up how far away you move from your dog to keep them engaged.
   - Don't always try to increase the distance in every session—sometimes take fewer steps to prevent frustration.

Final Tips for Both Sit-Stay and Down-Stay:

- Always vary the duration and distance to maintain your dog's interest.
- Be mindful of your dog's comfort and avoid training if it appears in pain, especially if lying down for long periods.
- If your dog starts getting up before you release it, just cue it back to the correct position and continue training from there.

Leave It/Take It Training

This behavior is essential for your dog's safety and could even save their life. When something falls on the floor, your dog may instinctively think it's theirs to eat or pick up. But what if it's something dangerous? It's far better to teach your dog to leave something alone rather than trying to take it away after they've already grabbed it or swallowed it.

The "Leave It" command is used when your dog is moving toward something you don't want them to touch. If trained properly, your dog will not touch the item at all. However, don't use the "Leave It" command after your dog has already grabbed something, as this is a different situation. Once your dog has something in their mouth, they can't "leave it." The cue should only be given before your dog touches the item.

Training this behavior may feel awkward at first because you'll need to hold both the clicker and treats in one hand, but with practice, it will become easier, and you'll soon replace the clicker with just the verbal cue.

The "Take It" command teaches your dog that it's okay to pick something up or eat it. Many dogs assume that anything dropped is theirs to claim, but this can be dangerous. By teaching the "Take It" cue, your dog will know when it's safe to take something and when it isn't. "Leave It" and "Take It" can be taught together.

Goal:
Your dog will leave items alone when cued and only take them when you say "Take It."

What You'll Need:
A clicker and treats.

Step-by-Step Training

1. **Start with Treats in Both Hands**
   Hold a bunch of treats in one hand and the clicker in the other. Keep your clicker hand behind your back so it's out of sight.
2. **Show the Treats**
   Show your dog the treats in your other hand. Immediately close your fist around the treats to prevent them from getting them, but don't pull your hand away—keep it right under their nose.
3. **Wait for the Head Turn**
   Be patient. Your dog may paw, lick, or try to grab the treats. Wait for them to move their head away from your hand.
4. **Reward the Right Behavior**
   As soon as your dog turns their head away from your hand, click and then toss a treat in the opposite direction. For example, if you were using your right hand, toss a treat with your left hand.
5. **Repeat**
   Repeat steps 1–4 for 10 repetitions and then end the training session.

Tips:

- Don't ask your dog to sit, lie down, or do anything else during this exercise. Focus entirely on the "Leave It" behavior.
- Click the moment your dog's head moves away from your hand, even if they look away for other reasons (like hearing a sound). The key is to reward the movement away from the temptation.

- Tossing the treat in the opposite direction helps reinforce the behavior of moving away from the temptation, which is useful if your dog is headed toward something dangerous.

Hand Placement

Keep your clicker and treats hidden behind your back to avoid distracting your dog. The goal is for your dog to leave the other hand alone, not be lured by it. If you drop something your dog shouldn't have, you won't always have treats handy, so you may need to wait to toss the reward until after you've clicked.

Progressing to the Next Step

When your dog is reliably moving away from the hand with treats, you can move on to the next stage.

1. **Reverse Hands**
   Repeat the previous steps but switch the hand holding the clicker. If you previously used your left hand, use your right for this round.
2. **Repeat**
   Do 10 repetitions and end the session.

When your dog reliably moves away from either hand, you can increase the challenge.

1. **Vary Hands**
   Switch hands during the repetitions. Do three repetitions with one hand, then switch to the other hand for two repetitions, and so on.

2. **Continue   Practice**
   Perform a total of 10 repetitions and end the session.

Training in Different Locations

Practice in different areas of your home, especially the kitchen or bathroom, where you're likely to drop things you don't want your dog to have.

Adding Cues

Once your dog is reliably leaving both hands alone, it's time to add verbal cues.

1. **Introduce   the   Cue**
   Have treats in both hands, with the clicker in one hand behind your back. Cue "Leave It" in a calm, friendly voice. Show your dog the treats in the other hand.
2. **Reward   the   Behavior**
   The second your dog moves away from the hand, click and reward them with the opposite hand.
3. **Repeat**
   Repeat this sequence at least twice.
4. **Add   the   "Take It"   Command**
   After your dog has left the treats alone when you cue "Leave It," add the "Take It" command when you present the treats. Then click and reward.
5. **Continue   Practice**
   Perform 10 repetitions and end the session.

Eventually, you won't need the clicker anymore, as the verbal cues "Leave It" and "Take It" will replace it.

Increasing the Difficulty

When your dog reliably responds to the "Leave It" and "Take It" cues with treats in your hand, increase the difficulty:

1. **Place a   Treat on   the   Floor**
   Cue "Leave It," then drop a treat about 12 inches from your dog, ready to cover it with your hand if they try to grab it.
2. **Wait   for   the   Behavior**
   Wait for your dog to leave the treat alone. The second they do, cue "Take It" and toss a treat in the opposite direction.
3. **Repeat**
   Repeat this for 10 repetitions and then end the session.

Over time, you can gradually reduce the need to cover the treat with your hand and increase the distance from which you drop it.

Dropping Treats from Height

As your dog progresses, start dropping treats from higher up to increase the challenge.

1. **Drop   Treats from   Different   Heights**
   Drop a treat from around an inch above the floor and cover it with your hand if necessary.
2. **Reward   and   Reinforce**
   When your dog leaves the treat alone, cue "Take It" and toss a treat.
3. **Practice**
   Repeat the steps for 10 repetitions, varying the height of the drop each time.

Eventually, you'll drop treats from greater heights and your dog will have learned to leave treats alone, even when they are on the floor or dropped from a height.

Tip:
As the height increases, it may become harder to cover the treat. If this happens, you can use your foot to cover it without kicking your dog, especially if they lunge for it.

By following these steps, you'll teach your dog to leave dangerous or inappropriate items alone and to only take things when you say so.

Chapter 11: Advancing Beyond the Basics

Once you and your dog have mastered the foundational commands, you can move on to refining them, gradually reducing the reliance on treats and the clicker, and begin working on more advanced behaviors. The great thing about dog training is that it's a lifelong journey; there's always something new to teach your dog. As you continue training, the bond between you will grow stronger.

Introducing Distractions

Your dog may reliably sit in the calm environment of your living room, but can he do the same in a bustling park? What if a dozen tennis balls are dropped around him? To solidify your dog's behavior, you need to introduce distractions, a process known as "proofing" the behavior.

The types of distractions you introduce depend on your training goals. For instance, if you plan to compete in dog shows, you'll need to expose your dog to distractions commonly found in such settings. These may include:

- Crowds of people
- Other dogs
- Being crated in a busy environment
- Loud noises
- Ring gates
- Mats
- A person moving near your dog while holding a clipboard

- Booths or tents
- Other dogs receiving attention and treats

If you aim to train your dog to become a therapy dog, he'll need to tolerate distractions like:

- People with unusual movements, such as those using crutches or wheelchairs
- People speaking loudly or slurring their words
- Beeping noises from medical equipment
- Slick floors
- Floor-length curtains (common in hospitals)

Consider your long-term training objectives when selecting distractions for your sessions. Whether you want your dog to perform reliably in competition, in new environments, or at a busy park, it's important to adapt distractions to match the situations you anticipate.

Start with small distractions and gradually increase the level of challenge. Here's an example of how to proof the Down command with distractions. This method can be applied to almost any behavior.

Goal: Your dog will remain in the Down position, even with distractions around him.

What You'll Need: Clicker, treats, regular leash, long leash (12 to 15 feet/2 meters), low-value toys, high-value toys, dog bowl.

Preparation: Ensure your dog has already learned the Down command.

1. Begin by warming up with a few repetitions of the Down command using the regular leash.
2. Swap the regular leash for the long one and repeat the Down command, gradually increasing the distance between you and your dog.
3. Cue "Down," and place one low-value toy in the training area, positioned far enough away that your dog can ignore it. If he stays in position, click and reward by tossing a treat away from the toy.
4. Repeat the previous step twice, each time moving closer to the toy.
5. Add a second low-value toy to the area and repeat the previous steps.
6. Now add a high-value toy to the area and continue practicing.
7. Add another high-value toy and continue to work your way closer, gradually increasing the level of distraction.

During future sessions, introduce more distractions like treats scattered on the ground, an empty dog-food bowl, or a bowl with treats in it. Only progress as far as your dog can successfully handle.

Tips: The introduction of a long leash itself is a distraction for your dog. It offers him more freedom and potential for distraction. Once he gets accustomed to this, start adding toys and food as distractions. Dogs are unique in what they find distracting, so learn what your dog finds most challenging and introduce those distractions later in the training. For particularly difficult distractions, offer a high-value reward when he ignores them.

When working in new areas, remember to start at an easier level and build back up. New environments can be full of new smells, sounds, and sights, which can make focusing difficult for your dog.

Off-Leash Training

If you want your dog to perform reliably off-leash, there are several steps to achieve this.

For behaviors like Watch Me, Walking Nicely on Leash, Sit-Stay, and Down-Stay, follow these general steps:

1. Start by practicing the behavior off-leash in a secure, enclosed area.
2. For behaviors where distance is important, such as Down, use a long leash initially. After successful long-leash training, you can transition to off-leash.
3. For behaviors that require your dog to stay close, such as Walking Nicely on Leash, use a short "tab" leash. This short leash allows you to maintain control while encouraging proximity. After successful training on the tab leash, move to off-leash.

Always check your local laws regarding leash requirements. If your area has leash laws, be a responsible pet owner and keep your dog leashed. Remember, while you may have trained your dog to be reliable, there may be an unexpected distraction that causes him to bolt. Assess the situation carefully before transitioning to off-leash training to avoid any risks.

When to Stop Using the Clicker

You won't need to rely on the clicker forever. Once a behavior is well-learned and consistent, you can phase out the clicker. Fluency means that your dog can perform the behavior reliably, even with distractions, in various locations.

If the behavior starts to break down or you encounter a new environment, you can reintroduce the clicker to strengthen the behavior again. For example, if your dog reliably sits at home but struggles to sit at a new location, using the clicker can help reinforce the behavior.

If too much time has passed since your last training session, you may need to use the clicker again to refresh your dog's memory.

Replacing the Clicker with a Release Cue

The clicker ends the behavior, but eventually, you'll want to teach your dog how to end the behavior without the clicker. This is where a release cue comes in.

The release cue tells your dog that the behavior is over. Without this cue, your dog may repeatedly perform the behavior or require multiple cues to stop. A release cue provides clearer communication.

Goal: Your dog will release from a position when cued, signaling the end of the behavior.

What You'll Need: Clicker, treats.

Preparation: Ensure the behavior is well-established first.

1. Choose a consistent release cue, such as "OK!" or "Free!".
2. Just before you click, give the release cue, then click and reward.
3. After about ten repetitions, phase out the clicker and use only the release cue.

When to Stop Using Treats

A common question in dog training is when to stop rewarding with treats. Stopping treats too soon can make training less motivating for your dog, which might cause him to lose interest.

That said, you don't have to rely on treats forever. Here's how to gradually wean your dog off treats while maintaining motivation:

Goal: Gradually reduce your reliance on treats while still rewarding the behavior.

What You'll Need: Clicker, treats.

Preparation: The behavior should already be fluent.

1. Start by rewarding with treats every other repetition of a behavior. For the repetitions without treats, use praise instead.
2. Gradually increase the number of repetitions between treats, sometimes rewarding after 3 or more repetitions.
3. Continue varying the intervals between rewards to keep your dog engaged.
4. After ten repetitions, end the session and repeat at different times, further reducing treat rewards until treats are no longer necessary.

Tip: If your dog loses interest or the behavior starts to break down, reduce the number of repetitions between treats or shorten the training session.

Building a Solid Recall

The Come command is essential for your dog's safety, especially in situations where there are distractions. A reliable recall can be challenging, particularly if your dog is distracted by something like a squirrel, which might be more enticing than you.

To achieve a reliable recall, consistency and patience are key. Here's how to polish the Come command:

Goal: Your dog will come when called, no matter the distraction.

What You'll Need: Clicker, treats, regular leash, long leash (12-15 feet/2 meters), low-value toys, high-value toys, dog bowl.

Preparation: Ensure your dog has already learned the Come command.

1. Warm up with a few Come repetitions using a regular leash.
2. Switch to the long leash and practice more Come repetitions.
3. Place a low-value toy in the training area, far enough that your dog can ignore it. Cue "Come!" If he approaches the toy, redirect him with the Come cue. Reward him with a treat when he reaches you.
4. Repeat the process, gradually getting closer to the distractions.
5. Add a second low-value toy and repeat.
6. Introduce high-value toys and repeat the exercise.

7. Continue adding more distractions, gradually increasing the difficulty.

The Joy of Heeling

If you want to take your leash walking to the next level, teaching your dog to Heel is essential. Heeling means your dog stays close to your left side, matching your pace, with his head turned toward you. It's a skill required in obedience competitions and other advanced dog activities like canine freestyle dancing.

Teaching Heel requires attention to both your and your dog's body position. You need to be mindful of your own movements to guide your dog effectively.

Heeling Basics

When teaching Heel, be conscious of your own body posture, as it directly influences your dog's position. For example, if you train with your body turned in a particular way, your dog will naturally mirror that. It's also important to consider your dog's physical comfort to avoid strain.

Clicker training is helpful here since it allows for short, effective sessions. Be careful not to overdo it, as too much repetition can cause strain for both you and your dog.

Goal: Your dog will walk in the Heel position with you, remaining by your side, focused on you.

What You'll Need: Clicker, treats, leash, long leash, any suitable distractions.

1. Start with the leash short enough that your dog is in the correct position when he's by your side.
2. Start walking and gently lure your dog back into position if he moves ahead.
3. Use the clicker to mark when your dog is in the correct position, and reward with a treat.
4. Gradually increase the duration of the walk before rewarding.

The Straight Sit

A key component of the Heel command is the Straight Sit. When a dog sits by your side, it's common for him to swing his rear outwards, which helps him see you more easily. While this is natural, in obedience competitions, you want your dog to sit straight, facing forward. Teaching this precise Sit behavior is a separate skill from the walking portion of Heel.

Goal: Teach your dog to sit straight, facing forward, by your side.

What You'll Need: Clicker, treats, and a long wall for training.

1. Stand with the wall on your left side, allowing enough space for your dog to sit comfortably between you and the wall. If needed, guide your dog to your left side. Cue "Sit," and when your dog sits straight next to your leg, click and treat.
2. Repeat this five times.
3. Step half a step away from the wall and repeat Step 1. If your dog continues to sit straight, without swinging towards the wall, click and reward. If he shifts or starts to lose the straight sit, move back closer to the wall. Perform nine more repetitions and end the session.

4. Gradually increase the distance from the wall while ensuring your dog maintains the straight sit. If he begins to swing out, step closer to the wall, repeat until he succeeds, and then try again from a further distance.

Once your dog is reliably holding the Heel position and looking up at you, and can sit straight by your side, it's time to combine these behaviors and add a cue.

Goal: Your dog will walk in Heel position, looking at you, and automatically sit when you stop.

What You'll Need: Clicker, treats.

1. Start with your dog sitting at your left side. Cue "Heel" in a friendly tone, and begin walking.
2. After a few steps, stop and cue "Sit." When your dog sits, click and treat.
3. Repeat this sequence five times, then end the session.
4. In the next session, repeat the sequence, but do not cue "Sit." Instead, wait to see if your dog automatically sits. If he does, click and reward. If he doesn't sit after a minute, cue "Sit." Continue repeating this process for a couple more sessions, gradually waiting for the automatic sit.

Next Steps

Once your dog can hold the Heel position for at least twenty steps in your training area, you can begin practicing in different locations. Keep in mind that you may need to revisit earlier steps when working in new environments, which is normal. If your goal is competition, practice in areas with mats and ring gates so your dog becomes accustomed to performing in those settings.

Gradually work toward your dog holding the Heel position for longer periods, but remember to keep training sessions short and minimize repetitions. If you wish to teach your dog to Heel on both sides, you can use a different cue for each side. This will help prevent strain on your dog's neck and joints.

If you haven't started off-leash training yet, now is the time to begin. Start in quiet areas and slowly move to places with more distractions.

Perfecting Your Steps

Your dog relies on your body cues to understand which direction you're going. To make your Heel more polished, be consistent with your body movements, especially when turning. This may take some practice, as you may not always be aware of what your body is doing when walking. For example, if your left foot leans slightly to the left before turning right, your dog might think you are turning left, causing him to lag behind on the turn. While this is fine for general walking, in a competition, it can cost points.

To improve, it's best to practice these movements without your dog first. Focus on getting your body used to consistent movements, and then add your dog. Here are some movements to help you and your dog walk together as a team:

- **Right Turn:** When you turn right and your dog is on your left, he will need to speed up on the outside of the turn to maintain Heel position. Signal the turn by stepping with your right foot slightly outward, then lifting your left foot and turning right. You can also drop your right shoulder slightly back.

- **Left Turn:** When turning left, your dog must slow down on the inside of the turn to stay in Heel position. To signal the turn, step with your left foot slightly outward, then lift your right foot and turn left. Dropping your left shoulder slightly back will help signal this turn.
- **About Turn:** In an About Turn, you turn to the right and circle around to continue in the direction you came from. This requires your dog to speed up to maintain Heel position. Signal the turn by stepping with your right foot slightly outward, lifting your left foot past your right, and completing the turn. You can also drop your right shoulder slightly back.
- **Figure Eight:** In obedience competitions, you'll need to perform a Figure Eight exercise, walking in a pattern that resembles the number 8 around two "posts." This will require more gradual turns, with your dog inside and outside of each turn. Use similar footwork as for the Left and Right Turns, but make the turns more gradual.

Chapter 12: Fun Tricks to Teach Your Dog

While certain behaviors are essential for teaching your dog basic family manners, others are simply for fun! Trick training offers a great way to break up your regular training routine. Some tricks, like *Fetch* and *Drop It*, can also be quite practical.

The process for training tricks is similar to teaching any other behavior. Below are twenty-five fun tricks you can teach your dog.

Back Up

Goal: Your dog will learn to walk backward away from you.

What You'll Need: Clicker, treats, and a narrow training area just slightly wider than your dog's shoulders. You could use a wall with a few chairs set up to create a narrow "hallway."

1. Stand close to your dog in the narrow space, facing them.
2. Take a small step toward your dog. Look for any backward movement, even if it's just one paw. When you see movement, click and treat.
3. Repeat, clicking and treating for any backward movement.
4. Once you reach the end of the "hallway," take a short break to reset and have your dog back up the opposite direction.
5. Repeat Steps 1-4 two more times, then end your session.

As your dog becomes more consistent, you can stop moving toward them. Instead, wait for them to step back without you advancing.

1. Stand in the same position and take a step toward your dog.
2. Hold still and wait for your dog to move back. When they start, click and treat.
3. Repeat until your dog moves several steps back on their own. Reset briefly when needed.
4. End the session after a few repetitions.

Once your dog reliably backs up without you stepping forward, add the verbal cue.

1. Cue "Back Up" in a friendly tone when your dog takes two steps backward, then click and treat.
2. Gradually increase the number of steps before rewarding.
3. Repeat until your dog moves backward the full length of your training area.

As your dog becomes confident, you can remove the barrier by gradually taking away parts of the "hallway" until they can back up freely. Eventually, the cue can transition to your release cue, "OK!"

Balance Bone on Nose

Goal: Your dog will balance a treat on their nose until you cue them to eat it.

What You'll Need: Clicker and treats that are easy to balance on your dog's nose.

Preparation: Teach *Sit-Stay* and get your dog accustomed to having their muzzle handled.

1. Cue your dog to *Sit*.

2. Gently place the treat on top of your dog's nose. If they try to grab it, pull it away. Wait for them to stay still, then click and treat.
3. Repeat until your dog remains still while the treat is on their nose.
4. Gradually increase the time the treat stays on their nose before clicking and rewarding.
5. Once your dog holds the treat steady, you can transition to a release cue when they're ready to eat.

Bashful

Goal: Your dog will place a paw on their nose, as if acting bashful.

What You'll Need: Clicker, treats, sticky note.

Preparation: Teach *Sit* or *Down* beforehand.

1. Cue *Sit* or *Down* and place a sticky note on your dog's muzzle.
2. Your dog will likely paw at the note to remove it. When they touch their nose, click and treat.
3. Repeat several times, gradually removing the sticky note once your dog is consistently pawing at their nose.
4. Add a verbal cue like "Are you bashful?" when your dog reliably touches their paw to their nose.

Crawl

Goal: Your dog will crawl on the ground.

What You'll Need: Clicker and treats.

Preparation: Teach *Down* first.

1. Cue *Down* and hold a treat just in front of your dog's nose. Slowly move it away from them a couple of inches, keeping it low to the ground. When your dog stretches toward the treat, click and treat.
2. Repeat a few times, rewarding each time your dog crawls toward the treat.
3. Gradually reduce the amount of treat movement and eventually work with an empty hand to encourage crawling.

Once your dog is crawling reliably, add the cue "Crawl" and a hand signal. Reward them as they complete the movement.

Dance

Goal: Your dog will stand on their hind legs and move in a circle.

What You'll Need: Clicker and treats.

Preparation: Make sure your dog is physically strong enough for this trick. It requires supporting their weight on their hind legs, so avoid this trick if your dog has any orthopedic issues.

1. Hold a treat above your dog's nose to encourage them to rise onto their hind legs.
2. When your dog's front paws leave the ground, click and reward.
3. Gradually move your hand in a circle to guide your dog in a full circle. Reward for every small movement.
4. When your dog completes a full circle, gradually build up to a longer routine.

5. Add a verbal cue, like "Dance," and reward them for completing the circle.

Drop It

Goal: Your dog will drop an item from their mouth when prompted.

What You'll Need: Clicker, treats, and an item your dog enjoys holding.

1. Offer your dog the item and let them hold it briefly.
2. Hold up a treat near their nose. When they drop the item to get the treat, click and reward.
3. Repeat a few times, then fade the treat in your hand until it's just a hand signal.
4. Once your dog is reliably dropping the item, add the verbal cue "Drop It."

Fetch and Retrieve

Not just retrievers can master this fun trick! The first step is teaching your dog to "Give," a skill you'll find detailed later in this chapter.

Goal: Your dog will retrieve an item, bring it back to you, and place it in your hand.

What You'll Need: A clicker, treats, and an item your dog is willing to carry in its mouth.

Preparation: Start by teaching "Give," as fetch involves a sequence of behaviors. It's easier for your dog to learn the final part—the "Give," or delivery to your hand—before tackling the full fetch.

1. Place the item on the floor near you.
2. Click and treat for any interest your dog shows in the item, even if it's just looking at it.
3. Repeat steps 1–2 for a total of 10 repetitions. Your goal is to get your dog interested enough in the item that it picks it up. This might not happen in the first session, and that's okay. If your dog does pick it up, it may spit it out when you click— and that's fine. The click ends the behavior, and you're rewarding the act of picking it up.

Once your dog is reliably picking up the item, it's time to add verbal cues.

1. Place the item near you.
2. Cue "Fetch" just before your dog grabs the item.
3. Cue "Give" right before your dog places the item in your hand. When they do, click and treat.

Repeat steps 1–3 for 10 repetitions. End the session.

In subsequent sessions, increase the distance between you and the item. If your dog drops the item too soon, backtrack to a point where the behavior was successful, and continue practicing from there.

Tip: As your dog becomes more reliable with fetching, practice in different locations and with a variety of items.

Give

The "Give" cue teaches your dog to place an item into your hand. This is the last step of the fetch/retrieve exercise and is useful in other scenarios, such as if your dog picks something up on a walk and you want it returned. With "Give," your dog learns that bringing you an item doesn't mean running away with it and being chased.

Goal: Your dog will place an item into your hand.

What You'll Need: Treats and an item your dog is eager to carry. You'll need two hands for this, so consider using a verbal marker like "Yes" instead of a clicker.

Preparation: First, teach your dog to "Take It."

1. Cue "Take It."
2. Hold one hand below your dog's muzzle and show a treat with the other hand.
3. When your dog drops the item to grab the treat, catch it. Mark "Yes" and reward with the treat.
4. Repeat steps 1–3 two more times.
5. Cue "Take It" again, but this time, hold your empty hand where the treat was, directly beneath your dog's muzzle.
6. When your dog places the item in your hand, mark "Yes" and reward.

Repeat steps 5–6 for 7 repetitions. End the session.

Once your dog reliably drops the item into your hand, it's time to add the cue.

1. Cue "Take It."
2. Just before your dog drops the item into your hand, say "Give" in a friendly tone, then hold your hand out. When they drop the item in your hand, mark "Yes" and treat.

Repeat this process for 10 repetitions, then end the session.

Over time, you can reduce the size of your hand signal and eventually rely on just the verbal cue. Start moving your hand a little to encourage your dog to approach and deliver the item.

Tip: Once your dog consistently responds to "Give," work with different items and gradually use lower-value objects, encouraging them to drop a wider range of things.

High Five

Teach your dog to give you a high five.

Goal: Your dog will raise a paw and touch it to your open palm.

What You'll Need: Clicker, treats, and a paw target.

Preparation: Before you begin, teach your dog to "Sit" and "Paw Target." Decide in advance whether you want your dog to use a specific paw for the high five.

1. Cue "Sit" and hold the paw target low in front of your dog, with your palm facing them. Cue "Paw."
2. When your dog touches their paw to the target, click and treat.
3. Repeat steps 1–2 for five repetitions, gradually raising the target so your dog has to stretch to reach it.
4. Once your dog is reaching for the target, hold your hand in the same position but without the target. Cue "Paw." If your dog touches your hand with their paw, click and treat. If they

don't, wait for about a minute, and try again. If they don't respond, go back to using the target.

When your dog consistently touches their paw to your palm, it's time to introduce the "High Five" cue.

1. Cue "Sit," then say "High Five" once, followed by "Paw." When your dog touches your palm, click and treat.
2. Repeat for a total of 10 repetitions.

In future sessions, use only the "High Five" cue, not "Paw."

Tip: Ensure your dog is sitting on secure ground to avoid slipping. Don't hold your hand too high or too low, and make sure your dog is balanced.

Jump Into Your Arms

If you're physically able and confident in your dog's ability, this trick will have your dog leaping into your arms!

Goal: Your dog will leap from the ground into your arms for you to catch.

What You'll Need: Clicker, treats, and a chair for you to sit on.

Preparation: Teaching "Wait" can help your dog learn to wait for the cue to jump.

1. Sit in a chair facing your dog.
2. Encourage your dog to jump into your lap. You can pat your legs and talk sweetly to them to get them to jump. When they

do, click and treat, then toss a treat on the floor to encourage them to jump down and reset.

3. Repeat for 10 repetitions, then end the session.

4. After 10 repetitions, when your dog jumps into your lap, briefly hold them in your arms. Ensure it's comfortable for both of you.

5. Repeat for 10 more repetitions.

6. Stand up and face your dog. Bend your knees and encourage your dog to jump into your arms. Hold them, click, and gently release them to the floor with a treat.

7. Repeat for 10 repetitions.

8. When your dog reliably jumps into your lap with your knees bent, cue "Hup!" or "Jump!" consistently and encourage them to jump into your arms. Click and treat for correct responses.

9. Repeat for 10 repetitions, gradually working toward a full standing position, rewarding successful jumps.

Jump Through a Hoop

Teach your dog to jump through a hoop for a fun and impressive trick.

Goal: Your dog will jump through a hoop.

What You'll Need: Clicker, treats, and a hoop large enough for your dog to pass through comfortably.

1. Hold the hoop in front of your dog on the ground. Click and treat for any interest in the hoop, even if they just look at it.

2. As your dog starts showing more interest, shape their behavior by rewarding them for placing one paw through,

then two, and finally all four paws as they pass through the hoop.

3. Repeat until your dog consistently goes through the hoop. Allow them to approach from both sides to avoid dependence on one direction.
4. When your dog is reliably passing through the hoop, cue "Through!" or "Hup!" and gradually raise the hoop a little higher with each repetition.

Teaching Your Dog to Recognize Toys by Name

You can train your dog to identify specific toys by name and retrieve them when asked.

Objective: Teach your dog to bring you specific toys upon request.

What You'll Need: A clicker, treats, and toys.

Preparation: Start by teaching your dog the "Fetch" or "Retrieve" command.

Step-by-Step Training:

1. Begin with a single toy (e.g., a tennis ball), placed at a short distance. Start with some basic fetch exercises, clicking and rewarding correct responses.
2. Label the toy by saying "Fetch Ball" as your dog retrieves it. Click and reward correct responses.
3. Repeat steps 1-2 for about 9 repetitions and then end the session.
4. Introduce a new toy, such as a squeaky bear, and follow the same process. Label it as "Fetch Bear" and repeat steps 1-3.

5. Place the tennis ball a short distance away and the squeaky bear around 2 feet (0.6 m) away.
6. Face the tennis ball and cue "Fetch Ball." If your dog retrieves the ball, click and reward. If your dog goes for the squeaky bear, move it further away and try again.
7. Face the squeaky bear, cue "Fetch Bear," and reward your dog when it retrieves the correct toy. If the dog goes for the ball, move it farther away.
8. Continue alternating between the toys randomly, repeating steps 6-7 eight more times. End the session.

In future sessions, gradually reduce the distance between the toys.

Tip: Once your dog reliably differentiates between two toys, introduce a third one. Follow the same process as with the first two toys, ensuring the dog is successful before progressing.

Paws Up

This behavior is helpful when you want your dog to place only its front paws on an object, such as a bed or your lap. It's particularly useful for therapy dogs.

Objective: Teach your dog to place its front paws on a person or object.

What You'll Need: A clicker and treats.

Preparation: Teach the "Paw Target" and "Off" commands first.

Step-by-Step Training:

1. Warm up with some Paw Target exercises.
2. Stand next to a bed or chair. Cue "Paw," click, and reward when the dog places its paw on the object. Follow with "Off," rewarding the correct response.
3. Repeat this process three times.
4. Once one paw is up, cue the other paw. Click and reward every correct response.
5. Repeat the previous step five times and end the session.
6. Now, with both paws on the object, withhold the click until the dog places both paws on it. Click and reward the correct response.
7. Gradually add the cue "Paws Up" before "Paw" in future sessions, transitioning to using only the new cue after ten repetitions.

Tip: Practice in different locations to generalize the behavior.

Play Dead

A fun trick where your dog will lie on its side and stay still, like playing dead.

Objective: Teach your dog to lie on its side and stay still when prompted.

What You'll Need: A clicker and treats.

Preparation: Teach "Down" and a release cue.

Step-by-Step Training:

1. Cue "Down." When your dog is in position, hold a treat near its nose and slowly move it under the chin and across the shoulder to guide the dog onto its side.
2. Once your dog is lying on its side, click and treat.
3. Repeat steps 1-2 twice.
4. Repeat the exercise with an empty hand, using the same gesture. Click and reward when your dog completes the side roll.
5. Repeat this seven times and end the session.
6. Gradually increase the time your dog holds the position on its side, up to about five seconds. Click and treat after each successful repetition.
7. Once your dog reliably stays on its side for five seconds, add the cue "Bang!" or "Play Dead!" just before the gesture.
8. Eventually, reduce the size of your hand motion until you can signal the behavior while standing.
9. Replace the click with the release cue "OK!" once your dog consistently performs the trick.

Put Toys Away

This is a helpful task where your dog will put its toys away in a box or basket.

Objective: Teach your dog to place toys in a designated storage area.

What You'll Need: A clicker, treats, toys, and a basket or box.

Preparation: Teach "Fetch" and "Drop It" first.

Step-by-Step Training:

1. Place the basket in front of you. Scatter toys around the room, not too far from you. Cue "Fetch." When your dog retrieves a toy, cue "Drop It," so the toy goes into the box. Click and reward.
2. Repeat the process until all toys are in the box. Click and reward every correct response.
3. Scatter the toys again and repeat the process for a total of ten repetitions. End the session.

In future sessions, gradually increase the distance from the box.

Roll Over

Teach your dog to roll over completely.

Objective: Your dog will roll over onto its side and return to its original position.

What You'll Need: A clicker and treats.

Preparation: Teach "Down" first.

Step-by-Step Training:

1. Cue "Down." Hold a treat near your dog's nose and guide it under the chin and across its body to encourage the dog to roll.
2. Click and reward when your dog rolls over.
3. If the dog does not roll all the way, reward any attempt toward the motion, gradually shaping the behavior.

4. After a few successful rolls, remove the treat from your hand but keep using the same hand signal. Click and reward each successful roll.
5. Repeat ten times and end the session.
6. Add the cue "Roll Over" just before you use the hand signal. Click and reward after successful attempts.

Shake Hands

Teach your dog to shake hands to show off its friendly side.

Objective: Your dog will place its paw in your hand for a shake.

What You'll Need: A clicker, treats, and a paw target.

Preparation: Teach the "Paw Target" command first.

Step-by-Step Training:

1. Hold the paw target in your hand, palm up. Cue "Paw."
2. When your dog places its paw on the target, click and reward.
3. Repeat the process twice.
4. Hold your hand without the target, cue "Paw," and reward when your dog places its paw in your hand.
5. Repeat this six times and end the session.
6. Add the cue "Shake" before "Paw" once your dog consistently offers its paw.

Sit Pretty

This trick involves your dog sitting up.

Objective: Your dog will sit up with its front legs off the ground.

What You'll Need: A clicker and treats.

Preparation: Teach "Sit" first.

Step-by-Step Training:

1. Cue "Sit." Hold a treat just above your dog's head, enticing it to reach up for it.
2. Click and reward as soon as the dog's front legs leave the ground.
3. Repeat the process twice.
4. Gradually reduce the need for a treat in your hand, just using the gesture. Click and reward correct responses.
5. Shape the behavior so your dog raises its front legs higher. Repeat this process six times.
6. Once your dog reliably sits pretty, add the cue "Sit Pretty" before rewarding.

Speak

Teach your dog to bark on cue.

Objective: Your dog will bark when you ask.

What You'll Need: A clicker and treats.

Step-by-Step Training:

1. Do something likely to make your dog bark, such as knocking on a door. When the dog barks, click and reward.
2. Repeat this five times.

3. Once your dog reliably barks in response, add the cue "Speak!" before rewarding.

Spin

Teach your dog to spin in a circle.

Objective: Your dog will rotate in a complete circle.

What You'll Need: A clicker, treats, and a target stick (optional).

Step-by-Step Training:

1. Hold a target stick at your dog's nose level and move it in a circular motion. Click and reward when the dog follows it in a complete circle.
2. Start with partial circles and gradually increase to a full circle, rewarding each successful attempt.
3. After ten successful spins, add the cue "Spin" just before you start the motion with the target stick.

Tip: If you want your dog to keep spinning, start rewarding after two or three spins. Use the release cue "OK!" to let them know when to stop.

Take a Bow

Teach your dog to bow after a performance.

Objective: Your dog will lower its front end while keeping its rear end up.

What You'll Need: A clicker and treats.

Step-by-Step Training:

1. With your dog standing, move a treat down between its front legs. When the dog lowers its head, click and reward.
2. Gradually shape the behavior so the dog bends its elbows, bowing its front end. Click and reward when it happens.
3. Once your dog is reliably bowing, add the cue "Take a Bow!"
4. Repeat until your dog consistently responds to the cue.

Up/Off

Teach your dog to get on and off furniture or you, with a cue.

Objective: Your dog will get off furniture or a person on command.

What You'll Need: A clicker and treats.

Step-by-Step Training:

1. Start by getting your dog on the furniture or your lap, using a cue like "Up."
2. Once on the furniture, cue "Off." Click and reward when your dog gets off.
3. Repeat this process five times.
4. Gradually introduce the cue for both behaviors, making sure your dog understands the difference between "Up" and "Off."

These tricks not only engage your dog physically and mentally but also strengthen your bond with them. Start with the simpler tricks and progress as your dog masters each behavior!

Chapter 13: Get Out There and Show Off Your Dog!

If you and your dog are enjoying training, why not take it a step further? There are so many fun activities you can do together! Many sports and events were originally designed for dogs bred for specific tasks, but today, both purebred and mixed-breed dogs are welcome to participate. No matter what adventure you pursue, make sure your dog is physically fit for the task and, most importantly, enjoying it.

Competing with Your Rescue Dog

If you adopted your dog, he might be a purebred or a mixed breed. While some dogs come with breed registration papers, many do not. In the past, mixed-breed or unregistered dogs had trouble entering competitive events, but that's no longer the case! For example, the prestigious Westminster Kennel Club Dog Show now allows mixed-breed dogs to compete in its agility events.

Today, many organizations accept mixed-breeds alongside purebreds. Whether your dog's pedigree includes a name like "Snowfall's Gallant Knight" or something more down-to-earth like "Hank," there's a place for him in the competitive world if you're both ready to participate.

Each organization has its own rules and registration process, so make sure to research how to get started. Don't worry about your dog's lineage—he can still become a champion!

Chapter 14: Handling Inappropriate Behavior

Ever find yourself yelling, "NOOOOO!" when your dog misbehaves? It's a natural response, but is it the most effective way to solve the problem? The short answer: No!

Yelling or physically punishing your dog may provide a temporary release for your frustration, but it's not a productive approach. For example, if your dog grabs your shoe and runs off, you might yell at him to come back, then scold him when he does. But in doing so, you might unintentionally teach him to avoid you next time or to hide with the shoe. This only reinforces negative behaviors.

Instead, consider more effective training methods. If you see him headed for the shoe, use a "Leave It" cue to prevent him from picking it up. If he's already holding the shoe, a "Drop It" command will encourage him to give it back.

If you haven't trained these behaviors yet, you can still handle the situation calmly. Encourage your dog to come to you, take the shoe away gently, and praise him for returning it. This teaches him that coming to you is a positive experience.

The Cost of Harsh Corrections

Dogs need rules and boundaries, but that doesn't mean you need to be harsh to be an effective leader. Using severe methods like swatting, yelling, or pulling on the leash may seem like a way to establish dominance, but these actions can cause fear and aggression in your dog, making things worse in the long run.

Examples of harsh corrections include:

- **Swatting or spanking**: This can lead to fear of hands and even aggression, and might teach your dog to avoid you.
- **Collar grabs**: This can make your dog fearful of being handled, and may lead to aggression, especially if someone reaches for his collar or head.
- **Alpha rolls (flipping your dog onto his back)**: This can confuse or frighten your dog and doesn't achieve the intended result. Dogs don't see this as a demonstration of dominance.
- **Yelling**: This can cause your dog to become fearful, not necessarily obedient. In some cases, it may cause your dog to growl in self-defense.
- **Spraying with water or vinegar**: This can create an aversion to water and may teach your dog to only obey when you have a spray bottle in hand.
- **Negative reinforcement**: Doing something unpleasant to force your dog to comply can result in fear, aggression, and a lack of trust. A "forced retrieve," for example, may get results but could lead your dog to dislike retrieving.

Instead, focus on positive reinforcement. Reward good behavior and manage undesirable behavior with gentle, proactive techniques.

Effective Discipline

If your dog does something you don't like, what should you do? The answer depends on the situation.

- **If your dog is about to hurt someone or himself**, a sharp "No!" can help interrupt the behavior. However, constant yelling loses its impact, so it should only be used sparingly.
- **If the behavior is simply annoying**, ignoring it can be very effective. Dogs dislike being ignored. For instance, if your dog is jumping by the door waiting for you to open it, don't open the door until he stops. This teaches him that bouncing around won't get him what he wants.

Managing and training your dog are the most effective ways to stop unwanted behaviors.

The Management Plan: Preventing Problems Before They Happen

Dog trainers often talk about the importance of management, and for good reason. Effective management prevents problem behaviors from becoming habits. The more your dog practices an undesirable behavior, the more ingrained it becomes. Teaching a puppy to walk nicely on a leash is much easier than retraining an older dog who has been pulling for years.

If your dog hasn't learned the appropriate behaviors yet, you'll need to manage his environment. If he's chewing inappropriate items, remove them until he understands what's okay to chew. If your puppy isn't house-trained, confine him until he learns where to go. The more behaviors you teach, the less you'll need to manage, and soon you'll have a dog who completely understands your rules.

Take Control

A humane and effective way to address misbehavior is by controlling the rewards in your dog's life. Once your dog learns that you control all the good things, he'll pay closer attention to you and start working for those rewards.

For example, if your dog shreds a toy, take it away—he loses that privilege. If he barks when you try to leash him, walk away—he loses the opportunity for a walk. If he pulls on the leash, stop walking—he loses the chance to explore. By withholding rewards, you teach him that these behaviors don't lead to anything fun.

Does the Devil Make Them Do It?

What causes your dog to misbehave? It's likely not what you think. Many behaviors such as barking, chewing, and jumping are simply normal canine behaviors. Dogs don't engage in these behaviors to "misbehave" but because they are naturally rewarding to them. It's your job to teach them when and where these behaviors are acceptable.

The Dominance Myth

One common misconception is that dogs misbehave because they are trying to be "dominant" or "alpha." The idea is that your dog wants to be in charge of the household, but this view overcomplicates things. Dogs don't spend their time plotting to overthrow you. They are simply responding to their environment and natural instincts.

The myth stems from outdated ideas about wolves, where an "alpha" wolf is seen as the leader of the pack. However, domestic dogs are not wolves, and their behavior isn't driven by a desire to dominate.

They do what they do because it's rewarding—chewing, jumping, and barking are behaviors that come naturally to them.

Even if your dog growls or challenges another dog for a spot on the bed, it doesn't necessarily mean he's trying to dominate you. He's simply protecting what he considers a valuable resource—his space.

Understanding Dog Behavior Triggers

Dogs often have specific triggers that influence their behavior. For instance, some dogs may bark excessively when they look out the window or when someone approaches their car. Others may growl when children approach, or only urinate inside the house during thunderstorms or fireworks. These behaviors can stem from either behavioral issues, such as fear, or from physical problems.

If your dog suddenly changes behavior, it's important to first rule out any physical health issues. For example, if your dog, who has been house-trained for years, starts urinating indoors again, a visit to the vet is recommended. Similarly, if a dog who has always been comfortable with being picked up suddenly snaps at you, a veterinary checkup is essential. Any physical problem must be addressed before you can begin working on behavioral solutions.

Once your vet confirms that there are no physical issues, you can start to explore other possible triggers. For example, have there been recent changes in your home that could be causing stress for your dog, such as a shift in your work schedule? Dogs thrive on routine, so even a small disruption—like coming home later than usual—can cause anxiety. When dogs are stressed, they may urinate or chew destructively.

If your dog exhibits undesirable behavior, ask yourself: "Is this normal? What caused it? Can I fix it?" While you may never have all the answers, making educated guesses can help you identify potential solutions.

Training Desired Behaviors

Once you've identified any triggers, you can focus on teaching your dog the behaviors you want to see. Instead of simply telling your dog "no" or reprimanding him, it's more effective to guide him toward behaviors you prefer. For instance, instead of constantly correcting your dog, train him to engage in a behavior that is incompatible with the undesired one. A well-chosen alternative can prevent the unwanted behavior from happening in the first place.

For example, if your dog tends to jump on guests, train him to sit calmly when visitors arrive. By encouraging incompatible behaviors, you're setting your dog up for success.

Helping Fearful Dogs

If your dog is scared of something, there are two main techniques that can help him build more positive associations with the feared object or situation. These techniques are also useful for dogs who dislike certain activities like nail trimming or bath time. For dogs exhibiting severe fear-related behaviors, such as urination or aggression, it's best to consult a professional who uses reward-based methods and has experience in handling such issues.

1. **Desensitization**
   Desensitization involves gradually exposing your dog to the feared stimulus at a level where he is aware of it but not

stressed. If your dog reacts negatively, you've gone too far and need to back off. For example, if your dog is afraid of the car, you might start by having him look at the car from a distance. As he becomes more comfortable, you can slowly decrease the distance, always ensuring that he remains calm. Desensitization can take a few sessions or many, depending on your dog's progress.

2. **Counterconditioning**
   Counterconditioning pairs something your dog likes with something he dislikes. For example, if your dog is scared of the car, you can give him treats every time he looks at the car. Over time, he'll begin associating the car with positive experiences rather than fear. It's important to move slowly and not overwhelm your dog; otherwise, you risk creating a negative association.

Both techniques are often used together for better results. By starting under the threshold where your dog is comfortable, rewarding calm behavior, and gradually increasing exposure, you can desensitize your dog while also counterconditioning his fear.

House-Training Challenges

House-training is one of the most common issues faced by dog owners, and many dogs are surrendered to shelters due to accidents in the house. However, house-training problems are often due to improper teaching, not the dog's fault.

Whether you're training a puppy or an adult dog, the process is largely the same. The main difference is that older dogs typically need fewer potty breaks than puppies. If your dog is having trouble with house-training, consider the following:

1. **Has Your Dog Ever Been Successfully House-Trained?**
   Has your dog ever gone three months without an accident?
   If not, he may not yet be house-trained.
2. **Is   the   Problem   New?**
   If your dog has been house-trained for a long time but has
   suddenly started having accidents, there may be an
   underlying cause.

If you're struggling with house-training, start by reviewing your
methods. Are you following the training plan carefully? Is everyone
in your household consistent with the rules? If not, inconsistent
training can confuse your dog and hinder progress.

Common Causes of House-Training Issues

1. **Too   Much Freedom   Too   Soon**
   If your dog has been given too much space before
   understanding where it's appropriate to eliminate, go back to
   stricter confinement and crate training. Gradually allow
   more freedom as he succeeds.
2. **Lack of   Supervision**
   Close supervision is key. If you're not watching your dog
   carefully, accidents are more likely. If you catch him before
   he has an accident, you can quickly take him to his
   designated potty spot.
3. **Insufficient   Potty   Breaks**
   Puppies, senior dogs, and certain breeds need more frequent
   potty breaks. Consider adding additional breaks to your
   schedule if necessary.
4. **Health   Issues**
   In some cases, house-training issues may be due to health
   problems. For example, excessive urination may indicate a

medical condition. If your dog's elimination habits seem abnormal, a visit to the vet is advisable.

Dealing with Confused Puppies

Some puppies take longer to grasp the house-training process. If your puppy is having trouble, try keeping a log of key details: when you give potty breaks, what happens during them, any accidents, and the puppy's feeding and water schedule. After tracking for a week, you may notice patterns that can help you adjust the training schedule. If your puppy seems to be eliminating excessively or has loose stools, a vet check is essential to rule out health issues.

Consistency and supervision are crucial. Celebrate every successful potty break with lots of praise and rewards. Some puppies take longer to understand the routine, but your persistence will pay off, ensuring fewer accidents as your dog matures.

Adult Regression in House Training

Occasionally, adult dogs who have been reliably house-trained for months or even years may experience setbacks. This is not uncommon during adolescence. If the issue arises suddenly, it's essential to consult with your veterinarian to rule out any health concerns. If your dog is cleared of medical issues, revisit the house-training process and start fresh as if your dog were a puppy. Most dogs tend to pick up the routine quickly once again.

Changes in routine can also confuse or stress your dog, leading to house-training regressions. For instance, moving to a new home or visiting someone else's house can trigger accidents. Just because your dog is house-trained in your home doesn't mean he knows the rules in a different environment. The previous inhabitants of your new home may have had a dog with house-training issues. Even though you might not be able to smell old accidents on the carpet, your dog can.

For example, a family moves into a new house and within a week, their previously house-trained dog starts urinating in the living room and hallway. After a vet check reveals no health issues, they suspect stress from the move. They begin confining the dog more and restart house-training, but the dog continues to have accidents. When they speak to their neighbors, they learn that the previous owners had an elderly Poodle who frequently urinated inside. The dog can smell these old spots and mistakenly believes it's an appropriate place to eliminate. If you suspect this, have the carpet professionally cleaned or even replaced if the problem persists.

If you're adopting a rescue dog that's said to be house-trained, it's still a good idea to implement a house-training program from day one. This will help set clear expectations for the dog. Being in a shelter can be stressful for dogs, so it's not surprising if a rescue dog has accidents. Shelter staff may have received incorrect information about the dog's training, or the dog might be too stressed from recent changes in its life to generalize house-training to all environments. Be patient and approach the situation as if you were training a puppy.

Submissive Urination in "Piddly Greeters"

Some dogs urinate when they greet people or other dogs, especially puppies or certain breeds like Cocker Spaniels. This is not a house-training problem, but a form of submissive behavior. The dog urinates as a way to show respect. It's more common in puppies and can be seen in some dogs that are particularly respectful or submissive.

This behavior might occur for various reasons: it could be because the dog respects taller people, men, or people with deep voices. While it might be messy, it's actually a sign of respect, so try not to get frustrated.

To manage submissive urination, follow these steps:

1. When you come home, ignore your dog for at least 10 minutes. Avoid eye contact and casual tasks like changing clothes or sorting your mail. This helps your dog calm down before you acknowledge him.
2. After 10 minutes, calmly let the dog out of his crate, but avoid eye contact and petting. Immediately take him outside to eliminate. Praise him for going outside and give him a treat.
3. Once back inside, ignore your dog for another 5 minutes.
4. Finally, you can acknowledge him. When you do, keep your greeting calm and low-key. Avoid leaning over him or petting his head, as this can be seen as assertive. Instead, try gently petting his chest.
5. When guests visit, consider confining your dog before they arrive to reduce excitement.

This type of greeting may feel unnatural, especially since you're excited to see your dog. However, the more exuberant your greeting, the more likely it is to trigger submissive urination. Once your dog learns that he doesn't need to show respect at all times, and once he gains better bladder control, you can gradually resume more enthusiastic greetings.

Marking in Adolescent Dogs

Marking is most common in adolescent male dogs, particularly those that are intact. Neutering early may help prevent marking, but if you haven't neutered your dog or are waiting for the procedure, marking may still occur.

Marking is essentially a house-training issue. As your dog enters the teenage phase, you'll need to remain vigilant. Testosterone levels are much higher in adolescent dogs than in adults—sometimes up to five times higher. This increase often triggers male dogs to begin lifting their legs and marking territory.

If your dog begins to mark inside the house, immediately interrupt him and rush him outside to his elimination spot. Praise him when he eliminates outside. If accidents occur inside, clean them thoroughly with an enzymatic cleaner to remove all scent markers.

Management can include using a belly band, which is a fabric wrap around the dog's belly and penis that holds a pad to absorb any urine. While this won't solve the underlying issue, it can help prevent marking when the dog is outside his familiar environment. The real solution is continued training and supervision.

Addressing Specific Behavioral Issues

Living with dogs can be incredibly rewarding, but it's not without challenges. Whether it's a house-training setback, attention-seeking behavior, or barking, there are effective ways to address these common issues.

Attention-Seeking Behavior

Some dogs learn to demand attention when they want something, often because their actions have been rewarded. For example, if your dog barks and you respond, he learns that barking gets him what he wants. Similarly, if he paws at you for attention and you respond, he'll continue the behavior.

One way to exacerbate attention-seeking behavior is by showering your dog with constant affection and attention, especially if you let him sleep in your bed. This can foster dependency and potentially lead to separation anxiety.

To address attention-seeking behavior, stop rewarding it. Initially, this will be hard, and your dog may escalate his efforts. Behavior often intensifies before it diminishes, but don't give in. Instead, focus on providing attention only when the dog exhibits appropriate behavior, such as when he's calm and relaxed.

Incorporating regular training sessions will help your dog learn that he gets your attention through positive behaviors rather than constant demands.

Barking

Barking is a natural dog behavior, but it can be disruptive if it's excessive. Dogs bark for many reasons, such as alerting you to something, fear, playfulness, frustration, or boredom. Identifying the cause of your dog's barking is crucial to addressing it.

If your dog barks when looking out the window, blocking his access to the window can help resolve the issue. If your dog barks out of excitement or frustration, you can train him to stop barking on cue using a clicker and treats.

Begging

Dogs may beg for food because they've learned that it's rewarding. If you've ever fed your dog from the table, he may associate your dining time with getting treats. To stop this behavior, ensure that no one in the household feeds the dog from the table. Instead, train your dog to go to a designated spot (like a mat or bed) while you're eating, and provide him with a food-stuffed toy to keep him occupied.

Car Anxiety and Carsickness

Some dogs experience nausea and stress during car rides. If your dog shows signs of anxiety, talk to your veterinarian about possible treatments. Gradual training, such as short trips and positive reinforcement, can help acclimate your dog to car rides.

Chasing and Herding

Some breeds are instinctively driven to chase or herd. Training your dog to "Leave It" can help prevent unwanted chasing behavior. You can also redirect his energy by providing chase-related toys, such as a flirt pole.

Counter-Surfing

If your dog can reach the counter, he may start investigating. Prevent counter-surfing by managing access to the kitchen, removing tempting food, and training your dog to focus on appropriate behaviors, such as redirecting attention to chew toys.

Digging

Just as some dogs are naturally inclined to chase, others are instinctively driven to dig. Terriers, for instance, were originally bred for hunting and killing vermin, so digging was an essential trait for chasing mice and voles. For many dogs, digging is also simply fun. It's impressive to see how two small paws can create such deep holes! However, this behavior can be frustrating and destructive for owners.

To stop your dog from digging, constant supervision is crucial. You need to interrupt and redirect the behavior in the moment. If you're not around to supervise, you can't effectively teach your dog to stop digging. One solution is to bring your dog inside when you're not home. If you're concerned about accidents or destruction indoors, consider crate training.

When your dog is outside, redirect his energy towards more desirable activities. Offer toys and rotate them frequently to keep him from getting bored and returning to digging.

Door-Darting & Escaping the Yard

Dogs often escape because it's an exciting adventure. The world beyond the yard is full of new smells and experiences. Unfortunately, once a dog learns that escaping is rewarding, it can be hard to break the habit.

Door-darting, or dashing out through gates, is easier to manage than when a dog escapes unattended from the yard. To prevent this, you can teach your dog behaviors that make escaping less appealing, such as the "Wait" command, where your dog has to wait for you to signal him before going outside. A "Down-Stay" on a mat or his bed is another effective command for times when someone arrives at the door. Simply having your dog sit before opening the door can also prevent a dash for freedom.

When a dog escapes from your yard, it becomes a more dangerous and difficult issue. The behavior is rewarding to the dog, but it can lead to life-threatening situations like getting hit by a car. To manage this, keep your dog inside when you're not home. Reinforce your fence to prevent escape; if your dog is digging under it, bury chicken wire several feet into the ground. If he's climbing over it, string wire across the top through PVC piping so that his paws slide off rather than finding a foothold. Make your yard more appealing by providing toys and rotating them regularly.

Eating Inappropriate Things (Coprophagia and Pica)

Some dogs have a habit of eating non-food items, such as poop or random objects. Coprophagia, the consumption of feces, is common, especially in puppies. Mothers lick their pups to stimulate elimination and clean them up afterward, which can lead to the habit. Some dogs outgrow this behavior, while others continue it into adulthood. A dog may follow another dog around, waiting to eat their feces as soon as it's deposited.

There are various theories as to why dogs engage in coprophagia, such as nutrient deficiencies or overly rich diets causing undigested nutrients to be present in the feces. However, no scientific evidence has confirmed these ideas. The only way to stop this behavior is by preventing your dog from eating feces. When you are outdoors, pick up feces immediately, or leash your dog if he's too quick to snatch it. Ensure your dog is on a balanced, easily digestible diet to reduce his interest in feces. Teach him the "Leave It" command to stop him from eating things he shouldn't.

Pica, the compulsion to eat non-food items like rocks or dirt, can occur due to boredom or lack of supervision. Some dogs may develop a dangerous obsession with eating non-food objects, which could lead to serious health risks, including blockages that may require surgery. If your dog is prone to eating inappropriate things, create a safe environment for him. Supervise closely and provide a variety of appropriate toys to keep him engaged. Rotate the toys regularly to prevent boredom and teach the "Leave It" command.

If you suspect your dog has a compulsive disorder, consult your vet for guidance.

Excitability & Nervousness

Some dogs are so energetic and excitable that they may seem like they have Attention Deficit Hyperactivity Disorder (ADHD). This tendency is often breed-specific. For instance, a Boston Terrier is likely to be more excitable than a Basset Hound.

To manage excitability, ensure your dog gets regular, adequate exercise, such as playing fetch, going on brisk walks, or interacting with another dog. Missing exercise time can lead to more hyperactive behavior. Additionally, teaching your dog to relax is just as important. You can schedule training sessions at times when your dog is naturally more tired. Start by giving your dog some exercise to help burn off excess energy, then settle down with him for a soothing massage. Start with short sessions and gradually increase the duration as your dog learns to relax.

Teaching commands like "Down-Stay" can also help your dog learn to settle down. Reward him with a food-stuffed toy when he relaxes on his bed, mat, or in his crate.

If your dog appears hyper due to nervousness, look for signs of stress, such as lip licking, whining, or trembling. In this case, you may need to address his anxiety triggers. Relaxation exercises can still help with nervous dogs, but it's crucial to identify and work through his specific fears.

Fear

Fearful dogs may show anxiety, and this can be a result of genetic factors or a lack of proper socialization during puppyhood. Signs of fear include cowering, whimpering, lip licking, yawning, and even urination. A dog that is fearful may also display trembling, turn away from the source of fear, or leave wet paw prints.

Socializing puppies properly during their critical socialization period can prevent or reduce fear. For adult dogs, desensitization and counterconditioning techniques can help them overcome fear. If your dog's fear is severe and affecting his quality of life, it's advisable to consult with a professional trainer experienced in working with fearful dogs.

Tools such as the Thundershirt (a snug-fitting jacket), Rescue Remedy (a Bach Flower Remedy), or dog-appeasing pheromones (DAP) may provide comfort in times of extreme stress. Medication prescribed by a veterinarian may also help balance a fearful dog's chemical imbalance and improve the effectiveness of behavior modification.

Never force a fearful dog to confront his fears, as this can backfire and cause further anxiety or aggression. Instead, gradually expose your dog to triggers in a safe, controlled manner while providing positive reinforcement.

Fear Biting

Fear-based aggression can lead to biting. A fearful dog may bite to defend himself if he feels threatened. It's important to work with a professional trainer who uses positive reinforcement methods to help modify this behavior. Protect your dog from situations where he feels threatened, especially around people who cause him anxiety.

If your dog is prone to biting, limit his interactions with people who frighten him, and avoid forcing him into uncomfortable situations. Work with a trainer to help your dog become more confident and learn to trust people in a controlled, positive manner.

Jumping on Furniture

While it's tempting to let your dog enjoy the comfort of the furniture, it's important to set clear boundaries. If you don't want your dog on the furniture, make sure the rules are consistent from the start. Don't allow him on sometimes and get upset with him at other times.

If your dog jumps on furniture when you're not around to supervise, you can block access or cover the furniture with boxes or other objects. Train your dog with the "Off" command to encourage him to get down. You can also use the Hand Target or the "Leave It" command to redirect him.

For dogs that are allowed on the furniture, teach them to only jump up when given permission. Place a blanket on the furniture and train your dog to settle on it using the "Down" command. If your dog jumps on furniture without permission, use the "Off" command and guide him to the right spot.

Jumping on People

Many dogs jump on people as a form of greeting, which is a natural social behavior. When a dog jumps on you, it typically indicates that they are friendly and excited to see you. However, this behavior is not always welcome, and it's important to ensure you're not accidentally rewarding your dog for jumping. For instance, if your dog places its paws on you while you're sitting on the couch and you pet them, you're inadvertently reinforcing the jumping behavior. Similarly, if your dog jumps on you while standing and you push them off or give them any attention, you are still rewarding the behavior. Some dogs find jumping fun and will continue to do it if it's encouraged, even unintentionally.

To address this, you need to teach your dog an alternative behavior that you prefer, such as sitting. You can train them to automatically sit when they greet people.

Goal: Your dog will automatically sit when approached by others.

What You'll Need: A clicker, treats, and other people to practice with.

Preparation: Teach your dog to sit.

Steps:

1. Have someone approach your dog. As the person gets closer, cue your dog to "Sit." The person should not pet your dog during this time. Once your dog sits, click and toss a treat to reset them for the next repetition.

2. Repeat this process nine times. Finish your training session after this.
3. In future training sessions, aim for your dog to automatically sit when a person approaches.

Once your dog consistently sits on their own, it's time to progress.

1. Have a person approach your dog. Your dog should automatically sit. Allow the person to let your dog sniff their hand and then briefly scratch behind their ear. After a couple of seconds of petting, click. Toss a treat to reset your dog for the next round. Ensure the person stops petting immediately when you click.
2. Repeat this nine times. End your training session.
3. In subsequent sessions, increase the duration your dog can remain sitting while being petted.

Tips: Only practice this with people your dog feels comfortable with. If your dog is fearful, do not make them sit when strangers approach, as this can cause anxiety or defensive behavior.

Mounting/Humping

Mounting, or humping, is a natural behavior in dogs that can be embarrassing in social situations. Dogs of both sexes, even if spayed or neutered, can display this behavior. It can occur during play, out of excitement, or even frustration. While humping can sometimes be sexually motivated, it is not always the case.

If your dog begins humping, calmly remove the object or dog they're humping. Giving attention to the behavior only reinforces it.

For instance, if your dog humps a toy, take it away and redirect their attention to something else, like a chew toy or food-stuffed toy.

If your dog is humping another dog, use the cue "Leave It" and separate them. If your dog humps a person, remove them from the situation. If the behavior is triggered by excitement, try to identify the triggers and manage the situation before it escalates.

Mouthing/Nipping

Puppies often mouth as they teethe or engage in play. However, mouthing can continue into adulthood if not properly addressed, and this can become problematic, especially with larger dogs. Some dogs may mouth when they're excited, such as when a retriever excitedly grabs your arm. While this might not bother you, others may be startled or frightened by it.

If your dog mouths you due to excitement, use the cue "Leave It" and redirect them to a suitable toy. If the mouthing continues, confine them until they calm down. Additionally, if your dog is mouthing to get attention or something they want, avoid rewarding this behavior. Instead, reinforce more acceptable behaviors, like "Sit" or "Down-Stay."

If your dog's mouthing is becoming aggressive or too intense, consult a professional trainer using reward-based techniques.

Phobias

A phobia is an extreme fear response. When a dog experiences a phobia, they may panic and act erratically, even putting themselves in dangerous situations like running into traffic or jumping through glass doors. Common phobias include fear of thunderstorms, fireworks, or certain household items, and can result in destructive behavior or self-injury.

Addressing Noise Phobias:

Even confident dogs can develop phobias, especially to loud noises like thunderstorms or fireworks. To help your dog overcome this, you can desensitize them by playing sound recordings at a low volume and gradually increasing it as they become accustomed to the noise. Always pair this with positive reinforcement, such as treats.

It's also possible that dogs are reacting to changes in barometric pressure or static electricity rather than the noise itself, particularly during storms.

Household Items:

Dogs can also develop fears of everyday household items like vacuums, hairdryers, or hoses. If your dog is afraid of something, don't force them to face it, as this can worsen their fear. Instead, help them learn to approach and tolerate the object in a controlled and positive manner.

Goal: Your dog will learn to approach and feel more comfortable around a previously feared object.

What You'll Need: A clicker and treats.

Steps:

1. Place the object at a distance where your dog isn't showing signs of stress. If the object makes noise, ensure it's turned off.
2. Watch for any interest your dog shows in the object. If they even glance at it, click and reward. As your dog shows more interest, continue to click and treat for each step closer to the object.
3. Repeat the process nine times. End the training session after this.
4. In future sessions, continue rewarding your dog for moving closer to the object and gradually build their confidence.

Once your dog approaches the object with confidence, begin to add movement or noise in small increments. Always keep the training sessions calm and short to prevent overwhelming your dog.

Resistance to Handling

Some dogs don't like being touched in certain areas, such as their paws, ears, or mouth. This is common, but it's important to address this behavior so you can care for your dog properly. Forcing them to endure handling could damage your relationship and increase their resistance.

Instead, teach your dog to tolerate handling in a positive way. Review the handling exercises in the Puppy Training section for a structured approach. Be patient with adult dogs, as it may take longer to change their mindset, but it is possible.

Be mindful of not teaching your dog to associate handling with negative experiences. For example, if you grab their collar to punish them or end a fun activity, they will learn to fear collar grabs.

Instead, teach your dog to come to you and sit calmly when you need to handle them.

Separation Anxiety

Separation anxiety is a distressing condition in dogs, where they experience intense fear when left alone. This anxiety can be so severe that dogs may injure themselves in an attempt to escape their confinement. It's important to note that separation anxiety is a serious disorder that requires proper attention and care.

While many people believe their dog has separation anxiety when they show signs of stress as they leave, this isn't always the case. A little stress doesn't necessarily mean the dog has true separation anxiety. The condition should be diagnosed by a veterinarian. Some of the key symptoms include:

- **Drooling**: When you return home, you may find puddles of drool on the floor, which may initially be mistaken for urine due to its appearance, but it will not have the usual urine smell.
- **Self-injury**: Dogs with separation anxiety may harm themselves trying to escape confinement.
- **Anorexia**: A dog with separation anxiety might refuse to eat when you are gone. Even food-stuffed toys may be ignored until you return.
- **Destructive behavior around escape routes**: Destruction often occurs around doorways or windows as the dog tries to escape. While general destruction may be seen in dogs that aren't suffering from separation anxiety, it's the focus on escape areas that marks this condition.

Treatment typically involves a combination of medication prescribed by your vet and behavior modification. Depending on the severity of the condition, it might require the help of a professional trainer, veterinary behaviorist, or a certified applied animal behaviorist. Successful treatment demands time, patience, and consistent effort. It's critical that the dog is not left alone during the treatment process, which can be a challenge for many pet owners. However, with the right approach, improvement is certainly possible.

There are also things you can do to help or hinder your dog's progress. For example, if your dog is extremely clingy, avoid letting him sleep in your bed. Some dogs become overly attached when allowed to sleep in such a privileged, scent-rich space. If your dog has behavioral issues, like fear or aggression, it's best to address those first before allowing him to sleep on the bed again. Even after the issue is resolved, continue to monitor him closely.

Another thing that can worsen separation anxiety is showering your dog with excessive attention. Overprotective behavior can make a dog feel insecure, as he might not understand why you are so anxious or smothering. If your dog has separation anxiety, take a step back and examine your interactions with him. You might have unknowingly contributed to the problem by being overly indulgent. While your love for your dog is genuine, it's essential to maintain healthy boundaries to prevent reinforcing insecurity.

Training is another valuable tool. By teaching your dog basic commands like "Sit," "Stay," or "High Five," you can help boost his confidence. Dogs suffering from separation anxiety often lack confidence, so any opportunity to build their sense of security can be helpful in the long run.

Shyness

Some dogs are not necessarily fearful, but rather shy or reserved, especially in new environments or around unfamiliar people. Shyness is not the same as outright fear, though it can sometimes manifest in similar ways.

If your dog is shy, it's important to recognize signs of stress, such as lip licking, yawning, hesitation, or clinginess. Dogs might also display displacement behaviors, which are perfectly normal actions that seem out of context. For instance, if you're about to take your dog into a pet store and he suddenly starts scratching at his collar, it's probably not because he has an itch, but because he's feeling stressed.

When your dog is stressed, try to identify the cause and allow him to adjust at his own pace. Don't force him into uncomfortable situations. Review tips on managing fear and phobias for additional strategies, as they can also help shy dogs. Additionally, desensitization and counter-conditioning techniques may be beneficial, especially if your dog is only shy in specific circumstances (e.g., around men). You could pair the presence of men with something positive, like your dog's favorite treats, to help him associate them with pleasant experiences.

Stealing

Dogs steal items because they find it rewarding. Whether it's food, toys, or something they're not supposed to have, stealing results in a reward, such as eating the item, being chased, or getting to chew on it.

A good management plan can prevent a lot of stealing. Don't give your dog access to things you don't want him to take. This may mean teaching your family to put away their belongings and ensuring you do the same.

While you're managing your dog's access, also teach him commands like "Leave it" when he approaches something you don't want him to have. "Drop it" is another useful command if he already has something in his mouth and you want him to let go. You can also teach your dog to "Retrieve" if you want him to bring you an item.

Whining

Whining can be especially frustrating, as some dogs are particularly skilled at producing high-pitched sounds that can be grating to the ears. While some pet owners don't mind barking, whining can often be more difficult to tolerate.

Dogs whine for various reasons. They may do so when they are stressed, anxious, or excited. Some dogs whine in an attempt to appease their owners when they sense tension. In some cases, whining is simply a characteristic of the dog's personality.

If your dog is whining due to stress, try to figure out what's causing it. Yelling at him will likely make things worse, so instead, review strategies from the Fear and Phobia sections for tips on managing stress. Even if your dog's anxiety isn't as extreme as that of a more frightened dog, similar approaches can still help.

Importantly, avoid rewarding the whining behavior. If your dog whines to get out of his crate and you let him out, or if he whines for a toy and you give it to him, you're reinforcing the behavior. Wait until he's quiet before giving him what he wants. This includes not rewarding whining that happens when your dog sees something outside and wants attention.

It's important to note that comforting a dog who is afraid is entirely different from reinforcing whining. Fear is an emotion, not a behavior, and comforting a fearful dog will not reward his fear. On the contrary, showing him that you are a safe and supportive presence is essential in helping him cope with his anxiety.

Chapter 15: Aggression

Aggression is one of the most distressing, frustrating, and intimidating challenges dog owners can face. It can be so upsetting that many owners refuse to acknowledge their dog's aggressive behavior until it escalates beyond their control. Common justifications include, "He must have been abused before we got him, so he doesn't like men," or "He didn't mean to bite me; I could tell he regretted it." While puppies are not always aware of the harm their bites can cause, adult dogs are fully capable of using their teeth purposefully. When a dog bites or snaps, it is not by accident—they mean it. Dogs have incredible precision and speed with their teeth, and it's unlikely you'll be fast enough to avoid it. If your dog misses, it's because he intended to, and if he bites, he meant to do so.

Aggression can manifest in several ways:

- **Growling**: Growling over food, toys, or a spot on the bed is a form of aggression. Growling when approached by a child is also a sign of aggression.
- **Barking and lunging**: These are common indicators of aggression.
- **Piloerection**: When the fur on your dog's back rises, it could signal aggression.
- **Snapping and biting**: These behaviors are clear signs of aggression.

Seeking Professional Help

If your dog displays any of these signs, do not wait to seek help. Aggression does not resolve on its own and tends to worsen over time. The best course of action is to get professional assistance, as aggression is complex and carries significant risk. Choose a trainer who uses reward-based methods, avoiding outdated techniques like choke chains, prong collars, or shock collars, as these can exacerbate aggression.

It's crucial to select a trainer with proven expertise in handling aggressive dogs. Be sure to interview them to verify their qualifications. A qualified trainer will guide you through a behavior modification plan, ensuring that you follow it properly. If children are involved, it is wise to consult a veterinary behaviorist or a Certified Applied Animal Behaviorist (CAAB). These specialists have different training than regular trainers, even those with excellent credentials.

If your dog is showing aggression toward children, seek immediate help. Consult your veterinarian for a referral to a behaviorist, even if it means traveling to find one. Many offer virtual consultations through Skype or phone calls.

General Tips for Managing Aggression

1. **Acknowledge the problem**: Recognizing that aggression is an issue and admitting it is the first step toward resolving it. It can be difficult to accept that your dog may not be perfect, but doing so is necessary for addressing the problem. Aggression does not mean your dog is inherently bad, and euthanasia is not the only option. Positive reinforcement training has made resolving aggression more achievable than ever.
2. **Don't punish growling**: Many owners mistakenly punish their dogs for growling, thinking it's a sign of misbehavior.

However, growling is a warning that your dog is upset or uncomfortable. If you punish your dog for growling, you risk eliminating the warning signal without addressing the underlying cause of his distress. It's better to hear a growl than to have your dog skip the warning and go straight to biting.

3. **Avoid physical punishment**: Physical punishment, like hitting or harsh corrections, will only escalate aggression and worsen the problem. Treat aggression with understanding, not aggression. Responding with forceful actions will likely make your dog more anxious and defensive.

Territorial Aggression

Territorial aggression occurs when a dog defends an area he considers his own. Some dogs may attack or bite anyone who enters the house, while others may act aggressively if someone enters the yard. Some dogs also exhibit territorial behavior around their car or crate. Studies have shown that dogs kept on chains in yards are more prone to territorial aggression.

While some people may tolerate or even encourage territorial aggression, it's important to note that dogs can't differentiate between threats and non-threats. If your dog is aggressive toward visitors, he might behave the same way toward a neighbor's child as he would toward an intruder.

Local laws vary on the owner's liability if a dog injures someone on their property, so be sure to familiarize yourself with local ordinances. Even if you're not legally responsible, the emotional impact of an injury caused by your dog would be devastating.

Sometimes, what appears to be territorial aggression may be fear-based. A dog who is barking and growling at visitors might not be protecting his territory, but instead, he could be frightened of people and trying to get them to leave. The key difference is that fear-based aggression can occur outside of the home, while territorial aggression is typically confined to a specific area.

Managing Territorial Aggression

When dealing with territorial aggression, management is key until you can implement a behavior modification plan with a professional trainer. Here are some management tips:

- Ensure that your fence is tall and secure. Consider adding a lock to prevent unauthorized access.
- Avoid using underground shock fences, as they can escalate aggressive behavior, particularly in territorial dogs.
- If you know guests are coming over, confine your dog until they've settled. Once your guests are comfortable, if your dog has accepted visitors in the past, bring him out on a leash for better control. Use treats and a clicker to reward calm, social behavior.

Training for Crate or Car Aggression

If your dog is protective of his crate or the car, here's a training exercise you can use to reduce aggression:

Goal: Your dog will not exhibit aggression when people approach his crate or your car.

What You'll Need: Treats and a helper.

Steps:

1. Have your helper walk past the crate or car, several feet away.
2. As soon as your dog notices the person, start feeding him treats, even if he growls or lunges. If he's too agitated to eat, move the person further away and try again.
3. Once the person has passed and your dog can no longer see them, stop feeding treats and ignore your dog.
4. Repeat this process 19 times, then end the training session.

Tips: The goal is to change your dog's response to people approaching his crate or car. By feeding him treats while the person is in sight, he will begin to associate the person's approach with something positive (food) instead of something threatening. Over time, his reactions will become less intense as he learns to anticipate rewards rather than feeling anxious about the approaching person. It may take several sessions depending on how long your dog has been practicing this behavior.

Aggression Toward People

Aggression in dogs is often rooted in fear. Dogs that are frightened of people may exhibit aggressive behaviors such as growling, barking, snapping, snarling, or biting. Simply punishing the dog won't eliminate the fear; instead, you need to teach your dog that people are safe and not something to fear. This process must be gradual and done carefully, ideally with the guidance of a professional.

Never force your dog to face his fears. Doing so can intensify his anxiety. For example, if your dog is scared of men, don't hand his leash to a man or force him to approach one. Even if the man is perfectly kind, to your dog, it may feel like you've handed him over to a "monster."

If your dog is aggressive toward strangers, put a solid management plan in place until you can seek professional help. Keep him away from unfamiliar people. When hosting guests, consider crating your dog, placing him in another room, or keeping him behind a secure baby gate to prevent overwhelming him.

If he's in his crate or behind a gate where you can easily control him, you can toss him treats while your guests are around. You might also give him a bully stick or a food-stuffed chew toy. Avoid letting your guests feed him treats, as a highly food-motivated but fearful dog could become overwhelmed. This might prompt him to approach a stranger for a treat but then feel uncomfortable with the close proximity, possibly resulting in a bite.

Aggression Toward Other Dogs

Some dogs are friendly with people but exhibit aggression toward other dogs. This can be driven by fear. Dogs that haven't been properly socialized with other dogs might feel threatened and react aggressively. Additionally, certain breeds were historically bred for dog fighting, and although dog fighting is now illegal, their genetic predisposition toward aggression may still exist.

While some dogs can learn to enjoy the company of other dogs, others may only tolerate them, and some may never be able to be around other dogs without displaying aggression. How a dog responds depends on individual temperament, early socialization, the length of time the dog has shown aggression, and the training methods used to address the issue.

Until you can get professional help, manage the situation carefully to avoid encounters with unfamiliar dogs. Taking your dog to a dog park to "socialize" him is not advisable, as it may exacerbate the aggression and create problems for the other dogs.

Resource Guarding

Aggression related to food, toys, or other items is known as resource guarding. Signs of this behavior include growling, tensing up when you approach, turning away from you, placing the item between you and the dog, carrying the item away, or eating faster.

While videos of dogs growling over objects are often posted online for amusement, these situations are not to be taken lightly. Even a small dog growling over a bone can bite. If the dog bites a child, the consequences can be severe. A dog growling over an object is showing stress and is signaling that he's upset. If you persist in trying to take the object, he might escalate the behavior and bite to communicate his discomfort.

If your dog growls over objects, start by making a list of all the items he guards and remove them from his environment until you can work with a professional. This list will help you understand which items to address first, starting with the least valuable ones.

For example, if your dog doesn't guard plastic chew bones but gets tense around tennis balls or growls over bully sticks, begin by working with the plastic chew bones. Here's how to start training:

Goal: Teach your dog not to resource guard.

What You'll Need: Treats and an item that your dog does not guard.

Steps:

1. Give your dog the item and let him chew on it for a few seconds.
2. Show him a treat. When he drops the item, immediately reward him with the treat.
3. Repeat this process 9 times and then end the session.

Tip: This exercise teaches your dog that dropping an item results in a reward. This lays the foundation for more advanced versions of this training, with the help of a professional trainer. The goal is to help your dog learn that sharing is okay.

Chapter 16: Solutions for Dealing with Rebellious Teen Dogs

If you've waited to train your dog until adolescence, or adopted an older dog, you're likely facing a challenging phase. Your dog may have developed undesirable behaviors over the months, and even if you started training early, you might now feel like your once-perfect puppy has transformed into a rebellious teen.

Shelters and rescues are often filled with adolescent dogs, as this phase can be tough for pet owners. Many people experience frustration when their seemingly well-behaved puppies turn into troublesome teenagers, leading to confusion and even abandonment.

Teen dogs require more supervision than when they were puppies. Their newfound energy and lengthened limbs allow them to reach places they couldn't before. Their speed makes them harder to catch, and suddenly, you're dealing with more trouble than you imagined.

While it's understandable to feel overwhelmed, giving up is not the answer. There are solutions to surviving your dog's teenage phase.

Understanding the Adolescent Phase

The best approach is understanding what's actually going on. Your dog is not deliberately rebelling; he's simply growing up. Adolescence brings a lot of changes, and your dog's senses become much sharper than they were as a puppy. They want to explore the world more actively, and their energy levels can be endless. Even if you think you've exercised them enough to wear out a marathon runner, they still seem to have more energy to burn.

Hormones play a huge role, especially in intact dogs. A dog overwhelmed by hormones is not always going to make the best decisions. For instance, a male dog might run straight into traffic following the scent of a female in heat without thinking to stop and look both ways. It's estimated that a dog can smell a female dog in heat from up to three miles away.

Male dogs can become obsessed with scents, especially where other dogs have marked, focusing entirely on the smell and not on your commands. It's not personal—it's just hormones at play.

Female dogs in heat can also become agitated and may become less responsive to your commands. Some may even experience false pregnancies, acting strangely by collecting toys and nesting. This can make your female dog act out of character.

Adolescence can also lead to irritability and snarkiness toward other dogs, even those they've previously gotten along with. Dogs of the same sex may begin to compete for attention or resources, particularly if there is a dog of the opposite sex involved.

As difficult as it may seem, remember that adolescence is just a phase. Just like puppyhood, it's a short blip in your dog's life. This too shall pass!

Training Troubles: What Happened to the Dog I Raised?

A common issue with adolescent dogs is that they may seem to forget all the training they've previously learned. You might have spent months teaching your dog, and then suddenly, when you ask them to "Down," they look at you like you're speaking a foreign language.

Don't be discouraged or angry. Your dog isn't ignoring you on purpose. Instead, take a step back in your training. Go over the basics and work from where your dog last performed well. You may need to start fresh, but don't worry—it won't take as long as it did during your original training sessions, and your dog will catch on faster because they already have that foundation.

New, Unwanted Behaviors

Adolescence is a time when dogs start to experiment with new behaviors, such as stealing socks or jumping on the couch. Some of these behaviors may be annoying, while others might cause more concern. For example, your dog might suddenly growl when you approach their bed or collar.

If your dog starts developing undesirable behaviors, training can help. For instance, if your dog begins stealing items, teach them to "Leave it." If your dog starts jumping on the furniture and you don't want that, teach them to "Down" or guide them to their bed. Always provide an acceptable alternative behavior for them to follow.

Fear Periods in Adolescents

Adolescent dogs can sometimes go through fear periods, where they exhibit irrational fears. Different theories exist about these phases, but many dogs experience a heightened sense of fear at various points during adolescence. You may notice that your dog suddenly becomes afraid of things that didn't bother them before. For instance, a dog who's used to seeing you pack a suitcase might suddenly bark at it when you bring it out, acting scared and defensive.

If this happens, don't panic—your dog may simply be going through a fear period. This is temporary and not a sign of rebellion. Fearful dogs are less likely to respond to commands, so be patient with them. Give it a few days, and check the fear section of Chapter 16 for tips on how to manage a fearful dog. Most dogs will bounce back from this phase in about a week, so try not to scold them during this time, as it will only make the fear worse.

Testing Boundaries

Adolescent dogs are constantly testing boundaries. What they were fine with as puppies may no longer be acceptable as teenagers. For example, your dog may suddenly decide to hop up on the dining room table or back away when you try to groom them, even though they've been brushed since they were young.

This phase isn't about domination; it's about your dog learning what they can and can't get away with. For example, if you throw a ball, and instead of bringing it back, your dog runs around the yard, you might find yourself chasing after them. This can lead to a cycle of "chase the dog" every time you try to put on a leash.

Rest assured, your dog isn't trying to dominate you. They're simply exploring their boundaries. Stay calm, return to training, and reduce their privileges until they learn the rules again. If your dog is interrupting dinnertime, revisit the "Down" command, or use crating or tethering to reinforce good behavior. If they don't want to be groomed, make grooming a more positive experience.

Most importantly, be consistent. If your dog is testing boundaries, you must re-establish the rules as if they were a puppy. Consistency and patience are key. Don't make the mistake of playing into their games, like chasing them around the house. Instead, teach them to sit when you attach the leash.

Remember, sometimes when dogs test boundaries or seem defiant, they may actually have a physical problem. If your dog suddenly resists grooming or stops on walks, there could be an underlying issue. Never assume it's stubbornness without first checking for physical causes. For instance, ear infections or hip dysplasia might cause discomfort that leads to behavior changes.

Helping Your Dog Through the Teen Years

The adolescent phase can either be a minor hiccup or a more challenging period. It really depends on your dog. But, with patience and understanding, you can survive this phase and help your dog grow into a well-behaved adult canine.

Here's a summary of key tips to help you navigate the transition:

- **Training**: Even if your dog is regressing in their training, revisit your lessons and commit to retraining. Consistency will help your dog catch up quickly.

- **Consistency with Rules**: Stick to your household rules without being harsh. Positive reinforcement will help your dog understand that following the rules is more rewarding than breaking them.
- **Manage and Redirect Behavior**: Adolescent dogs get easily distracted by smells and new experiences. Redirect their attention to more desirable activities, like rewarding them for coming when called, or using food-stuffed toys for positive reinforcement.
- **Patience and Understanding**: Your dog is not trying to be difficult or dominant. They're still your lovable puppy, just going through a phase. Avoid physical punishment, as it can lead to worse behavior. If you're frustrated, calmly crate or confine your dog until you can think things through.
- **Veterinary Assistance**: If your dog's behavior changes suddenly or you're puzzled by their actions, consult your veterinarian. A physical problem could be behind the behavior change.
- **Professional Training Assistance**: If you reach a breaking point, seek help from a professional, reward-based trainer. It's better to address issues early on before they become ingrained.

With these strategies, you'll be well-equipped to handle your dog's rebellious teen phase and guide them toward becoming a well-adjusted adult dog.

Chapter 17: Training a Rescue Dog

Rescue dogs are not "broken" or "damaged." They often end up in rescue for various reasons, most of which are simply because they behave like dogs. Unfortunately, some people have unrealistic expectations about how dogs should act, which can lead to their surrender.

One common issue is the lack of proper research before acquiring a dog. Many people fall in love with an adorable dog from a movie or commercial, only to find that when the puppy grows up, it exhibits typical dog behaviors—sometimes ones they are not prepared to handle. For example, someone who is not ready for the responsibility of a large dog, like a Mastiff, may be overwhelmed when the cute little puppy grows into a 200-pound adult. Dogs are a significant responsibility, both in terms of time and financial commitment, and many people aren't fully prepared for this when they bring a dog into their home.

In some cases, dogs end up in rescue due to life circumstances. If a family faces financial hardship or a senior owner passes away, the dog may be surrendered to a shelter.

Behavioral problems can also contribute to a dog being placed in rescue. Common issues include lack of housetraining, excessive rambunctiousness, and poor manners, such as jumping, mouthing, or pulling on the leash. Thankfully, all of these issues can be corrected with proper training. Some dogs may also have more serious issues like fear or aggression, often linked to past experiences. A reputable rescue organization will be transparent about any behavioral concerns, allowing potential adopters to decide if the dog is a good match for their home.

A challenge with adopting a rescue dog is that you often don't have full background information on the dog's past experiences. You may not know how they behave with children, whether they are house-trained, or if they have a history of biting. However, if the rescue uses foster homes, you may get a better sense of how the dog behaves in a home environment, though it's important to remember that every home is different.

Even if you don't know much about a dog's past, it doesn't mean you can't create a wonderful future together. Whether you adopt a puppy or an adult dog, there are ways to help your new companion adjust to their new life with you. For puppies, laying a solid foundation with training is essential, and for adult dogs, there are other considerations to help them settle in.

Bonding with and Socializing Your Adult Rescue Dog

Don't be surprised if your new dog doesn't listen to you at first. He may not have had training, or he might only respond to the person who previously trained him. Even if your dog greeted you like an old friend, it doesn't mean he has truly bonded with you yet. One of your first goals should be to build a strong, trusting relationship with your new dog. Spend time with him, play, and discover what he likes. For example, does he love squeaky toys but not tennis balls? Does he go crazy for liver treats but ignore cheese?

An effective bonding technique is hand-feeding your dog all of his meals. This establishes you as the source of something essential—

food—and helps the dog view you as an important figure in his life. It also creates positive associations with hands, making future grooming, medical care, and other interactions easier. If your dog is shy or fearful, hand-feeding can help him overcome some of his hesitations, as he'll begin to associate your presence with something positive.

Training is another excellent way to bond with your dog. It not only improves communication between you and your dog but also teaches him desired behaviors and rewards him for working with you. You don't need to wait to start training your rescue dog—once you identify what motivates him, you can begin.

Dealing with Bad Habits

Your new dog may have developed some habits that you don't like. For instance, he might have been allowed on the furniture in his previous home but you prefer that he stays off. He might jump on you or beg at the table, which can be frustrating. The good news is that these issues are usually solvable with training. Teach him alternative behaviors that you find more acceptable, and use positive reinforcement to help him learn new habits. Reviewing the "Basic Cues" chapter will provide helpful guidance.

The Importance of Structure

Bonding with your rescue dog doesn't mean you should immediately start indulging him, only to change the rules later. While it may be tempting to be overly lenient, especially with a dog who seems shy or has a rough past, dogs thrive on structure and routine. Establishing clear house rules from the start is crucial. For example, if you allow your new dog to sleep on the bed right away, but later decide you want him to sleep on his own bed, it will confuse him. Similarly, feeding him from the table because you feel sorry for him could encourage begging.

You can show love and compassion for your dog without indulging him. Setting and enforcing clear rules—using positive reinforcement to teach these rules—will help your dog settle into a healthy routine and prevent unwanted behaviors from developing.

Helping the Shy Dog

If your rescue dog is fearful or initially shy in his new environment, you can help him adjust by paying attention to what scares him and watching his body language for signs of stress. Reading about fear and phobias in Chapter 16 will teach you how to recognize these signs and manage them.

For example, your new dog may be hesitant to walk on hardwood floors, but fine on carpet. This is likely because he has never encountered this type of flooring before. You can help him by making the experience positive, using treats to reward any confident steps onto the floor. Gradually increase the exposure as he becomes more comfortable. Don't force him, but take small steps, always respecting his pace.

Introducing your shy dog to new people and environments can be overwhelming. Keep initial introductions brief and limited to one or two people at a time. Observe how your dog reacts and allow him to warm up at his own pace. If your dog seems more comfortable with certain people—perhaps he's shy around men—you can work on socializing him to feel less fearful.

Dealing with Common Issues

There are several common challenges that people experience with rescue dogs, and being aware of them can help you prepare for what's ahead.

Separation Anxiety

Rescue dogs, particularly those that have been abandoned or surrendered, can develop strong attachments to their new owners. If you spend a lot of time with your dog at first and then return to a normal routine, the shift might trigger separation anxiety. To avoid this, don't overwhelm your dog with too much attention at the beginning. Instead, give him time to adjust gradually. Start with short periods of separation and build up from there. Crate training can also be helpful for teaching your dog to be comfortable when you're not around.

If you notice signs of separation anxiety—such as clinginess, whining when you prepare to leave, destructive behavior, or refusal to eat—contact a professional to address the issue early before it becomes ingrained.

House-Training Issues

It's common for a rescue dog to have accidents in the house, especially if he wasn't properly house-trained in his previous home. Even if he was house-trained before, he may not apply that knowledge in a new environment. The best way to prevent accidents is to implement a consistent house-training program immediately, even if the dog seems to be house-trained. If he is already trained, the process will be quick. If not, this will help you establish good habits from the start.

By understanding and addressing these challenges, you can create a positive, fulfilling life for your rescue dog. With patience, love, and proper training, your new companion can become a well-adjusted and beloved member of your family.

Chapter 18: Training Senior Dogs

It's never too late to teach an older dog new tricks! In fact, senior dogs often have better focus and attention spans than puppies. Whether you're welcoming an older dog into your home or your long-time companion is simply getting older, it's always a great time to start teaching him new things.

Keeping the Mind Sharp

Training a senior dog is an excellent way to keep his mind active and stimulated. This is especially true if you've had your dog for many years and have already done various activities together. Perhaps your dog can no longer keep up with agility courses due to age, or maybe arthritis limits his ability to run like he used to. You might also have a new puppy that demands a lot of your attention. Even though his body may not be as agile as before, your senior dog likely still has the desire to stay involved. Teaching him new skills will help keep his mind sharp and give him something fun to focus on.

When choosing activities or tricks, make sure they're suitable for your dog's physical capabilities. If you're unsure, it's a good idea to check with your vet. Keep in mind that new activities don't have to be complex. Your senior dog can still learn simple tasks like retrieving the newspaper or picking up his toys.

Training Aids

As dogs age, they often experience a decline in their hearing, and they may develop arthritis or other physical issues. Here are some ways to adapt your training and communication methods for a senior dog:

- **Use hand signals**: If your dog's hearing is starting to fade, you can use hand signals instead of vocal cues. You may find that he can still hear high-pitched sounds like a clicker, but if not, try using a visual marker instead. For instance, you can start with a closed fist, open it to reveal all five fingers, and then close it again. Follow the signal with a treat to help him associate the new visual cue with positive reinforcement.
- **Scent-based games**: If your dog's vision is declining, you can still engage him in games that rely on his strong sense of smell. For example, you can play a variation of the shell game by hiding a treat under one cup. When your dog noses the cup, lift it so he can access the treat. Once he gets the hang of it, add more cups to increase the challenge. This will encourage him to rely on his sense of smell to find the treat.
- **Dog ramps for easier travel**: If you still like to take your senior dog on trips, consider using a dog ramp to help him get in and out of the car. A portable ramp will make it easier for your dog to travel with you, without straining his joints from jumping in and out of the vehicle.

Cherishing Your Bond

As your dog ages, those little gray hairs on his muzzle are reminders of all the time you've spent together. Take lots of photos and videos to preserve the memories. All the love, training, and time you've shared have created a special bond. Through positive training methods, you've nurtured a relationship built on respect and affection. What a beautiful journey you've both had!

Glossary

Behavior: Any action or activity that an animal performs.

Bite inhibition: The process by which an animal learns to control the force of its bite, avoiding hard or painful bites.

Capturing: A training technique in which you mark and reinforce a behavior that the dog naturally performs, without using any lures.

Classical conditioning: A process where a neutral stimulus is paired with an involuntary response, eventually causing the neutral stimulus to trigger the response on its own.

Clicker: A small, handheld device that makes a "click" sound when pressed, used as a training tool to mark desired behaviors.

Clicker training: A method of training that uses a clicker to indicate when a dog has performed the desired behavior, followed by positive reinforcement.

Conditioned response: A learned reaction to a previously neutral stimulus that now triggers an automatic response.

Conditioned stimulus: A stimulus that was once neutral but, after being paired with an unconditioned stimulus, begins to evoke a conditioned response.

Counter-conditioning: A technique where a negative or undesired stimulus is paired with a positive one to change the animal's response to the original stimulus.

Cue: A verbal or physical signal used to prompt a dog to perform a specific behavior.

Displacement signal: A normal dog behavior displayed out of context, often as a calming or "cutoff" signal.

Dominance: A relationship dynamic in which one individual asserts control, typically through aggression or force, to claim priority access to resources such as food, space, or mates.

Fluency: The level of mastery in a behavior where the dog can perform it reliably in different environments, with distractions, and under various conditions.

Luring: A training technique where you guide a dog through a behavior using a reward or object, without physical contact.

Marker: A signal, often a sound like a click, used to immediately mark the desired behavior so the dog understands what action is being reinforced.

Modeling: A technique that involves physically guiding a dog to perform a behavior, often by manipulating the dog's body.

Negative punishment: A training method where something enjoyable is removed following a behavior, decreasing the likelihood of that behavior occurring again.

Negative reinforcement: A technique where an unpleasant stimulus is removed after a behavior, increasing the chances of the behavior being repeated.

Operant conditioning: A learning process in which the animal's behavior is influenced by the consequences (reinforcements or punishments) that follow it.

Pheromones: Chemical signals emitted by animals that influence the behavior or physiology of other animals.

Piloerection: A condition in which a dog's fur, usually on the shoulders or back, stands on end. This can occur in response to fear, aggression, or heightened excitement.

Positive punishment: A technique where an unpleasant stimulus is added following a behavior, leading to a decrease in the frequency of that behavior.

Positive reinforcement: A method in which a favorable or rewarding stimulus is given after a behavior, increasing the likelihood that the behavior will occur again.

Shaping: A training technique that involves reinforcing successive approximations of a desired behavior, gradually moving closer to the final behavior.

Target: An object or location that an animal is trained to touch with a part of its body, such as a nose or paw.

Target stick: A long stick, sometimes telescopic, used in target training, where the dog is taught to touch the stick with its body.

Made in United States
Cleveland, OH
23 March 2025

15451713R00115